Just Jeeves

Life lessons from the
end of a short leash

as recounted by
Kathy Dorsey

Copyright © 2019 by Kathy Dorsey
First Paperback Edition

All rights reserved. No part of this publication may be reproduced, distributed, or transmitted in any form or by any means, including photocopying, recording, or other electronic or mechanical methods, without the prior written permission of the publisher, except in the case of brief quotations embodied in critical reviews and certain other noncommercial uses permitted by copyright law. For permission requests, write to the publisher, addressed "Attention: Permissions Coordinator,"
at the address below.

Published by Freiling Publishing, a division of Freiling Agency, LLC.

70 Main Street, Suite 23-MEC
Warrenton, VA 20186

www.FreilingPublishing.com

Library of Congress Control Number: 2019906294

ISBN 9781950948024

Printed in the United States of America

DEDICATED TO:

The Downtown Dogs

ACKNOWLEDGMENTS

Jeeves and I are grateful for the support of our family, particularly my husband Terry Dorsey, and our friends - you know who you are. You make our writing journey worthwhile.

We are also grateful to Editor Carol Feineman of the *Lincoln News Messenger* who gave us the opportunity to write the "Scene to be Seen" weekly columns in which Jeeves appeared and the *Just in from Jeeves* bi-weekly columns. Thank you for your editing and advice.

Our appreciation extends to authors Lora Finnegan and Jeri Chase Ferris (www.jerichaseferris.com) who filled in for Jeeves during our vacations in both the *Lincoln News Messenger* and our weekly blog *Just in from Jeeves*.

We wish to thank Kevin Gallagher who set up the original *Just in from Jeeves* website and posted our weekly blogs; the late Jack Wartleib who helped make the site come more alive with his many photographs of Jeeves; and, attorneys Therese Adams and Marilyn Clark who edited the weekly blogs.

We also wish to thank Editor Noreen Skillman who published *Just in from Jeeves* weekly blogs through the Internet newspaper, *The Lincoln Beacon*, and the Internet publication, *Now Lincoln*, along with Shelly Ebenholtz who posted a hyperlink to our weekly blog through the Lincoln Hills Yahoo Group.

And, we would like to acknowledge the assistance we received from City of Lincoln Public Information Officer Jill Thompson and former Lincoln City Clerk Patricia Avila.

On a personal note, I would like to thank Sue J. Clark, Bonnie Dunlap, Andy McMurtrie, Beth McMurtrie and Arloa Walter of our *Artist Way* study group. You inspire me.

Lastly, Jeeves and I are happy that we found Tom Freiling of the Freiling Literary Agency. He encouraged us to sort and compile 7 years of columns and blogs into this book that we call *Just Jeeves*.

Cheers!

Jeeves and Kathy Dorsey
2019

TABLE OF CONTENTS

FOREWORD 1
A NEW DAWN, A NEW DAY.... 2
HANDS FREE.... 5
ACTUARIALLY SOUND... 7
A NEW PATH.... 8
BAA, BAA BLACK SHEEP.... 11
FEROCITY.... 13
TAXING.... 15
TIMES ARE CHANGIN'... 17
TOUGH ENOUGH.... 20
A LONG LIFE SHORT-LIVED... 22
HAPPINESS IS.... 24
IF ONLY.... 26
ENCHANTING.... 29
BACK OF THE PACK.... 31
WEIGHTY MATTERS.... 33
THE SNIFF TEST.... 36
INTRANSIENT... 39
PAINTED BLACK.... 42
SMALL MERCIES... 45
DECISIONS, DECISIONS... 47
SEATBELTS FASTENED.... 49
SIZE DOESN'T MATTER.... 52
LINE TIME.... 54
'TWAS... 57
IN A LAND CALLED HONNAH LEE... 58
BY A NOSE... 60
PROBLEMATIC... 63
HOLES IN ONE... 66
HOME AGAIN... 69
BEWARE OF PINK... 72
BED TIME.... 74
WALK WAYS.... 76
MAKE MINE A DOUBLE.... 77

SWING AMONG THE STARS…	80
IT'S TIME…	83
FOUR-STARS…	86
CARE, CUSTODY AND CONTROL…	89
MUSIC TO HIS EARS…	91
BEST IN SHOW…	94
THE WRITE STUFF…	98
PET PEEVE…	100
WATCH WHERE YOU HANG YOUR LEASH…	104
A LEAGUE OF THEIR OWN…	107
THINKIN' LINCOLN…	111
THE LONG AND THE SHORT…	114
LET 'EM EAT CAKE…	117
WE THE PEOPLE…	120
CONFUSION…	123
TAKING STOCK…	125
R-E-S-P-E-C-T…	128
EYESORE…	130
DESPITE IT ALL…	133
TABLE FOR TWO…	135
MAKING THE GRADE…	138
WHAT PRICE BEAUTY…	139
I LOVE YOU BUT…	142
GLORY BOUND…	146
OLD ELEPHANTS…	148
SUBPLOT…	152
NO MAN, NO DOG…	154
FAIRY TAILS…	157
NOT IN VAIN…	160
AUDITIONS…	162
NEW TRICKS…	165
MINUTE BY MINUTE…	167
LEST WE FORGET…	171
DOGGED…	173
NO BONES ABOUT IT…	175

GIMME SHELTER…	178
ON YOUR HEELS…	180
VISIONARY…	183
NEWS VERSUS VIEWS…	184
SIMPLY THE BEST…	187
THE NEXT FOUR YEARS…	189
COMIC RELIEF…	193
PERSPECTIVE…	196
TRICK OR TREAT…	198
WORLD VIEW…	201
DOGS' BEST FRIEND…	204
COMMENTERRIER…	206
TRAIN OF THOUGHT…	209
S'IL VOUS PLAÎT…	212
ABOVE AVERAGE…	215
A MATTER OF STYLE…	217
SCRATCH AND SNIFF…	220
HIS TREE…	223
LIGHTING STRIKES…	225
TO BE OR NOT TO BEE…	228
MUTT AND JEFF…	231
LAST FOR BEST…	233

🐾 FOREWORD

Jeeves is a Yorkshire Terrier. Although he has a British pedigree, Jeeves was born in Lincoln, California where he spent most of his life together with Kathy and Terry Dorsey. They lived in a home that was located in a Lincoln development called Sun City Lincoln Hills. Two years ago, Jeeves, Kathy and Terry moved to Summerfield, Florida.

Even though Jeeves likes living in Summerfield, Jeeves loved living in Lincoln. And, Downtown Lincoln inspired him. In particular, Jeeves loved spending around the fountain in Beermann Plaza. While there, he often met up with the Downtown Dogs. Like any Terrier, Jeeves was easily distracted. The Downtown Dogs kept Jeeves on track. As a result, he was able to come up, together with Kathy, columns about the people, events and politics that shaped the city. These columns appeared in the *Lincoln News Messenger* under "Scene to be Seen" and "Just in from Jeeves." He also came up with weekly blogs that appeared on the website called, *Just in from Jeeves*. Alas, the original website no longer exists.

Kathy was inspired by reading books. Two books, in particular, inspired her. The first book was Stephen Leacock's *Sunshine Sketches of a Little Town* that she read in the eighth grade. The second book was Richard J. Needham's *Needham's Inferno* that she received as a fifteenth birthday gift from her aunt, Gweneth R. Myke. While both Leacock and Needham were humorists, their types of humor are vastly different. Yet, both authors captured the essences of a small town and a big city, respectively. It's the essence of a small city that Kathy, writing, as Jeeves, attempted to capture when she wrote "Just in from Jeeves."

Unlike Jeeves, Kathy was born in Toronto, Canada. She has no pedigree. Kathy spent most of her life in cities other than Lincoln including Richmond Hill, Brampton, Peterborough, Whitby and Toronto which are located in the Province of Ontario, Canada. She has also lived in Chicago which is located in the State of Illinois; Walnut Creek which like Lincoln, is located in the State of California; plus Longwood and Daytona Beach which, like Summerfield, are located in the State of Florida. Residency in those cities taught Kathy that the issues we face are the same regardless of a city's size or its landmarks. Residents of Lincoln face the same concerns as residents of any other North American city.

So, when you read the following columns and blogs, which can be read in any order, it may benefit you to substitute your town or your city for the City of Lincoln. Additionally, it may benefit you to substitute the names of any people referenced, such as the names of Lincoln's politicians, with names of comparable people in your town or city. And, most importantly, if it benefits you, Jeeves hopes that you will substitute his name for the name of your dog.

🐾 A NEW DAWN, A NEW DAY....

Jeeves looks forward to every new year.

He's excited about the possibilities that each one brings.

For him, this year is no different than last year.

It represents new beginnings.

Jeeves was disturbed when he saw a recurring Facebook post.

In it, viewers were asked to stay up past midnight on Dec. 31 so they could watch 2016 die.

Jeeves wondered what it was about the past 12 months that disappointed Facebook subscribers.

He understands that many were saddened by the deaths of celebrities such as Leonard Cohen, David Bowie, Prince, George Michael and others.

Jeeves admits that he was saddened by a celebrity death too.

He mourns the passing of Sutter, Governor Brown's Pembroke Welsh Corgi that served as the state's first pooch.

He also suspects that others may have become tired of the elections and, in particular, the results.

Jeeves admits that it seems to take forever to complete our elections.

Perhaps it's because candidates start new campaigns so soon after the last one has ended.

According to news reports, many people are unhappy with the results of our national election.

Jeeves knows many people who are unhappy with the results of our city election.

He doesn't know why they're unhappy.

Did they want to clean the swamp, clean house or just want someone new?

Jeeves is prepared to accept the results, move on and celebrate all that life has to offer.

Jeeves is reminded of a song called "Feeling Good."

The song was written by Anthony Newley and Leslie Bricusse for the musical, *The Smell of the Greasepaint - The Roar of the Crowd.*

It was performed for the first time in 1964 by Cy Grant and has been performed by many other performers such as Sammy Davis, Jr., Nina Simone, Sheryl Crow and John Coltrane.

Jeeves' favorite version is by Canadian singer Michael Buble.

The lyrics include references to birds, sun, sky, fish, sea, stars, butterflies and a new world.

Nature always makes Jeeves feel good.

Jeeves especially likes the song's chorus:

"It's a new dawn
It's a new day
It's a new life
For me
And I'm feeling good
I'm feeling good."
"New" is a small word.
It contains just three letters.
Yet, it has countless meanings.
According to Google, it can mean:
- not existing before
- made
- introduced
- discovered recently
- now for the first time.
- recently developed
- up-to- date
- latest
- current
- state-of-the-art
- contemporary
- advanced
- recent
- modern
- cutting-edge
- leading-edge and more.

Jeeves knows that some will continue to mourn 2016 for a long time.

It's their prerogative.

But Jeeves is not going to attend any pity party for the past.

Instead, he will be out celebrating each and every new day of 2017.

Whenever possible, Jeeves spends his time around the fountain in Beermann Plaza.

There, he will savor all that Lincoln has to offer.

He hopes the Downtown Dogs will join him.

Jeeves will watch customers come and go from Simple Pleasures Restaurant.

He hopes that they notice the new wood floor and like it as much as he does.

As a dog, he can't go inside but he can appreciate the expense, time, effort and the new look.

Jeeves looks forward to the transformation of Foto's Market that the new owner plans.

He hopes that others will stop by to meet the new owner too.

As a dog, he can't go inside but he can appreciate new ideas for beverage and deli counters.

Jeeves looks forward to new displays by Art League of Lincoln.

He hopes Lincoln will turn out to support its artists too.

As a dog, he can't go inside but he can appreciate creativity.

Jeeves looks forward to new productions by Lincoln Theatre Company.

He hopes other will attend their performances too.

As a dog, he can't go inside but he can appreciate the smell of greasepaint and the roar of the crowd.

Jeeves will also watch the inauguration of our 45th president, Donald Trump, on television.

He hopes that others will watch too.

As a dog, he wasn't invited nor can he attend but he can appreciate new leadership and he's willing to give it a chance.

Jeeves will watch our Lincoln City Council on the second and fourth Tuesday of every month.

He hopes that others will watch too.

City Council now includes one new face.

As a dog, he can't attend meetings but he can appreciate a 20-percent change in leadership and the promise that someone with new ideas and perspectives should bring.

Jeeves looks forward to this new year.

For him, it represents a new beginning.

Despite what he sees on Facebook, he's feeling good.

Jeeves hopes that others are too.

🐾 HANDS FREE...

Jeeves has a new friend named Runt.

Runt is a Boer Market Goat.

Runt was introduced to Jeeves by Taylor Button.

Taylor is a student at Glen Edwards Middle School.

She is also a member of the Sheridan 4-H club.

Jeeves learned that 4-H clubs date back over 100 years.

The "H's" in 4-H stand for Head, Heart, Hands, & Health

Its website (4-h.org) shows that 4-H has now grown to become the country's largest youth development organization.

Sheridan 4-H Club meets at 7 p.m. on the second Thursday of the month in Stewart Hall, 6005 Camp Far West Road.

As a member of Sheridan 4-H club, Taylor has been learning more about raising and maintaining a healthy goat.

She feeds Runt grain and alfalfa hay.

Last weekend, Taylor showed Runt at the Gold Country Fair in Auburn where she placed fifth in Showmanship and received a blue ribbon in her market class.

When she reaches Lincoln High School, Taylor plans to enroll in agriculture classes.

Jeeves wishes that he could take classes with her.

Meanwhile, as a 4-H member, Taylor is acquiring other valuable skills.

In addition to agricultural advancements, 4-H club members also examine other important issues such as global food security and safety, climate change and sustainable energy.

Members, such as Taylor, also gain leadership skills as well as explore ways in which they can give back to their communities.

Jeeves is happy to show support for Taylor, her 4-H club and all the other 4-H clubs.

In addition to Sheridan 4-H club, there are 11 other 4-H clubs in our area.

Lincoln has two clubs - Flatlands 4-H Club and Mt. Pleasant 4-H Club.

Flatlands 4-H Club meets at 6:30 p.m. on the first Wednesday of each month in Superior Livestock Supply, 641 H Street.

The club has about 50 members.

Mt. Pleasant 4-H Club meets at 7:00 p.m. on the second Wednesday of the month in Mt. Pleasant Hall, 3333 Mt. Pleasant Road.

Last year, the club had about 25 members and looks to increase its size this year.

Jeeves wishes he could join a 4-H club.

But he's not eligible.
He has a head.
He has a heart.
He has health.
Alas, he does not have hands - he has paws.
However, he is happy.
Jeeves is happy to know Taylor and her goat, Runt.

🐾 ACTUARIALLY SOUND...

Jeeves likes to meet with the downtown dogs.

They like to congregate around the fountain in Beermann Plaza where they discuss local issues.

Seldom to they agree on everything.

It's to be expected.

They live in different parts of town, they are different breeds and they are different sizes.

Each has a different perspective, both literally and figuratively.

These differences make for lively debate and hard-won consensus.

As a result, Jeeves wonders how our City Council members can vote unanimously so quickly, after so little debate, on so many issues especially ones, like the budget, that are so contentious.

Jeeves decided to retain a consultant to find out why.

He contacted a widely-respected independent actuarial firm, Robertson Eadie Actuarial Associates, and asked them to calculate the probability of five people voting unanimously on every issue.

To assist the actuary with his calculations, Jeeves provided him with synopses of prior City Council meeting agendas and minutes.

Jeeves won't bore you with the actuarial calculations but he will share the results.

He found them interesting.

Based on "yes" or "no" votes with the potential for abstentions, the probability of five people voting unanimously is about 6 percent.

It's analogous to a coin-toss

To achieve 100 percent probability, he learned that they would have to be identical quintuplets who lived together in the same place without any exposure to any outside influences.

Jeeves has seen photographs of our council members in the newspaper.

He is certain they were not separated at birth.

Actuarially, he now knows that is more probable for unanimous votes 6 percent rather than 100 percent of the time.

Jeeves is gratified to learn that the downtown dogs follow the norm.

What he doesn't understand is why our council members fall outside the norm.

Maybe it's because they take the "Consent Agenda" literally rather than figuratively.

Or, maybe they're lemmings after all.

🐾 A NEW PATH...

Jeeves is a little dog at the end of a short leash.

Sometimes a leash is called a lead.

Jeeves doesn't know why it's called a lead because he doesn't get to lead.

Although he may be out in front on his walks, he doesn't set the path.

Someone else leads him.

One day, Jeeves hopes to be a leader.

Jeeves watches leaders in action and tries to learn from them.

He's doesn't know everything that it takes to be a good leader.

But, he does know that if you believe that you're leading and no one is following, you're not leading.

You're simply taking a solitary walk.

Jeeves has learned that some people are elected to lead.

These people have many followers who vote them into their leadership roles.

For example, our presidents and our state governors are elected into their leadership positions.

And, Lincoln's city Councilmen are elected into their positions.

Jeeves hears that some leaders are made.

Until recently, he didn't know how it's done.

But, by watching the March 26, 2015 city council meeting, Jeeves found out.

Lincoln has a new city manager.

His name is Matt Brower.

Mr. Brower joined the city February 9, 2015.

Over the past eight weeks, Jeeves watched Mr. Brower.

And, he's been learning about leadership from him.

What Jeeves finds interesting is that Mr. Brower does not consider himself a leader although he's this city's manager.

During city council meetings, Jeeves hears Mr. Brower say to city Councilmen "council leads, staff follows."

The first time Mr. Brower used this expression, Jeeves thought there must be some misunderstanding.

But, after Mr. Brower repeated this expression several more times, Jeeves believes that our city manager means what he says.

Jeeves finds Mr. Brower's approach differs from the previous city manager's approach.

After watching the former city manager during city council meetings over the past six years, Jeeves came to believe that the city manager led and our city council followed.

Based on what he's seen from our new city manager, Matt Brower, Jeeves has to come to believe that the reverse is true.

Jeeves likes the new city manager's approach.

Our city manager expects city council to lead and set direction.

It's a new concept for Jeeves.

And, it's a concept that he hopes takes hold.

Based on the events during the March 26, 2015 special city council meeting, his hopes may be realized.

The special city council meeting took place on the third floor of city hall.

Unfortunately, the meeting wasn't televised so Jeeves had to rely on the meeting agenda and minutes plus his notes.

The meeting agenda showed four items.

Item 1 was Roll Call.

Item 2 was Citizens Addressing Council.

City council opted to discuss Item 4 before Item 3.

Item 3 was a Water Master Plan Presentation.

Item 4 was a resolution about engineering services for the city's groundwater well 2.

City Manager Matt Brower and Interim Deputy Public Services Director Jennifer Hanson presented a report that covered background, analysis, options and their recommendation regarding well 2.

Their report was prepared within 48 hours of the March 24, 2015 city council meeting and in direct response to council's frustration over delays that could jeopardize $1 million in grant funding.

Following their presentation to city council, City Manager Matt Brower, again, reiterated "council leads, staff follows."

Jeeves found city council's discussion revealing.

And, he learned a lot about leadership.

Mayor Paul Joiner and Councilman Peter Gilbert wanted to show their support for the new city manager by giving the report their endorsement.

However, Councilmen, Gabriel Hydrick, Stan Nader and Spencer Short adopted another stance.

They discussed the report in many different ways.

And, they came up with another recommendation.

Jeeves wonders why Joiner and Gilbert were so ready to use their rubber stamp.

The new city manager has said time and again "city council leads and staff follows."

Jeeves takes him at his word.

Based on what he saw during the meeting, Jeeves believes that Councilmen Hydrick, Nader and Short also take Mr. Brower at this word.

Jeeves wonders what it is about the new city manager's approach that Mayor Joiner and Councilman Gilbert don't appear to understand.

Don't they know what it takes to lead?

Jeeves wonders if Mr. Brower will make leaders out of Mayor Joiner and Councilman Gilbert.

Will they accept the challenge and take action like Councilmen Hydrick, Nader and Short?

Or, will Mayor Joiner and Councilman Gilbert remain stuck in the past?

Will they remain bound by the old managerial style?

Right now, Jeeves doesn't know the answers to these questions.

Jeeves learned a lot about leadership by watching Councilmen Hydrick, Nader and Short on March 26.

He will have to wonder, watch and wait to learn anything about leadership from Mayor Joiner and Councilman Gilbert.

Meanwhile, Jeeves would like to invite City Manager Matt Brower to go for a walk.

He will be happy for Mr. Brower to take the lead.

And, Jeeves will be happy to follow him along a new path.

🐾 BAA, BAA BLACK SHEEP...

Jeeves likes to watch the sheep that have been grazing on the north side of Ferrari Ranch Road.

Some are white and some are black.

He wishes that he could join the sheep and the dogs that help shepherd them.

Alas, Jeeves is not big enough.

And he knows nothing about sheep.

Nor does he know how to shepherd.

At gatherings of large groups of people, Jeeves sometimes hears references to "black sheep of the family."

Yet when Jeeves sees these black sheep family members, they look nothing like the sheep he sees grazing.

A few of them might have long curly hair.

But they walk on two legs, not four.

And they speak.

They don't baa.

They look like people.

They look nothing like sheep.

Regardless, Jeeves discovered that being called a "black sheep of the family" is not a good thing.

He wondered why black sheep are undesirable.

After all, it takes a farmer as much time to raise a black sheep as it does any other sheep.

But Jeeves learned that the wool from a black sheep cannot be dyed.

So black wool can have lower market value.

As a result, many farmers view black sheep as worth less.

During the 1700s and 1800s, the color black was associated with the devil.

Back then, black sheep were seen as being marked by the devil and they were feared.

Based on what he found, Jeeves is now beginning to understand why some family members may be referred to as black sheep.

Their families perceive them as being worth less.

Or worse, being marked by the devil.

Jeeves is not sure which of these might apply.

But he learned that, today, black sheep are no longer feared.

And he learned that there are farmers who have worked for decades to develop sheep that produce only black wool.

Top-grade fleece, regardless of color, is always desirable.

Many fiber artists and other crafts people seek out dark fleece.

Once again, Jeeves discovered that perceptions can change over time.

And once again, he found that quality can be more important than quantity.

And quality can also mean greater value.

Based on what he has learned, the next time Jeeves hears any group refer to family members as black sheep, he'll think about them differently.

He knows that some families will always believe that they're worth less.

But Jeeves believes that maybe they just need a good shepherd.

🐾 FEROCITY...

Sometimes Jeeves fails to recognize the sounds of familiar footsteps as they approach his front door.

When this happens, he barks and growls.

By the ferocity of both, you might be tempted to think that Jeeves is a big dog.

But he is just a small dog on a short leash.

All the Downtown Dogs are bigger than him except for his new friend Lexi.

She's a Chihuahua.

The Downtown Dogs tell Jeeves that not everyone likes Kathy Dorsey's column, "Scene to be Seen" in the *Lincoln News Messenger* nor do they like Editor Carol Feineman and Reporter Stephanie Dumm.

Others have also made Kathy aware either during their visits to her clothing store or during her visits with other downtown business owners.

Jeeves understands.

He knows that some people don't like the color blue either.

Jeeves also knows that it's impossible to please all the people all the time

Newspaper columnists are no different.

What Jeeves doesn't understand are more serious accusations that he also hears.

Months ago, he heard people accuse *Lincoln News Messenger* of trying to destroy the city and other variations on the same theme.

More recently, Jeeves has heard the same accusations about members of Team Lincoln as well as citizens who support the recall of some city councilors.

He finds that they are usually leveled at individuals who ask uncomfortable questions or try to make a difference.

By doing so, these individuals upset the status quo which makes them more susceptible to all kinds of wild and wooly allegations even when all they want is the best for Lincoln.

Jeeves wishes to assure readers that neither he nor Kathy have any desire to destroy the city.

And he is certain that neither Editor Carol Feineman nor Reporter Stephanie Dumm have any ambitions to bring about Lincoln's ruination.

When Jeeves first heard the allegations, he thought that he should thank his accusers for imbuing them with such awesome powers.

Since then, he's thought long and hard about what would he do with power if he had it.

Jeeves believes that he would be running leash-free all around Beermann Plaza especially during this nice spring weather.

He also believes that he would be running a tab at Foto's Market.

Jeeves believes Kathy Dorsey would be enjoying the pride-of-ownership that comes with a chain of clothing stores throughout the world and hobnobbing with fashion designers like Vera Wang and Stella McCartney.

And, Carol Feineman would be acting as Editor-in-Chief of the *New York Times* where Gloria Steinem and Donald Trump would be begging her for interviews.

And, Stephanie Dumm would be enjoying accolades as a crack reporter for the *Los Angeles Times* where she would be covering press conferences with President Barrack Obama and flying with him on Air Force One.

Jeeves shared these beliefs with Kathy.

She informed him that his beliefs, although generous in spirit, miss the mark.

Kathy believes that Carol and Stephanie, like her, live and work in Lincoln because they already have the power to chose where they live and work.

Every morning they open their front doors and set foot in Lincoln to enjoy another day in this great city.

Eventually, they hope that everyone will become more familiar with their footsteps.

Then, they hope that there will be not only fewer but less ferocious barks and growls.

And Jeeves can continue to enjoy Beermann Plaza from the end of his short leash.

🐾 TAXING...

Jeeves learned that this time year is called spring — one of four seasons.

He also learned that this time of year is called tax season.

Jeeves has found that tax season creates anxiety.

He overheard someone quote Benjamin Franklin to whom it is attributed, "In this world, nothing is certain but death and taxes" (*Bartlett's Quotations*).

Jeeves can't imagine equating death with taxes.

Perhaps that's why there's anxiety.

On Sterling Parkway, Jeeves has observed a young man dressed up as the Statue of Liberty.

He's promoting the services of a tax-preparation company.

Jeeves hopes that this company can liberate everyone from the fear of death due to taxes.

In Jeeves's household, tax filings are prepared by a certified public accountant.

Sometimes, accountants are called bean counters.

Jeeves wondered what types of beans they count.

He has heard of lima beans, green beans, fava beans and jelly beans.

Jeeves could find no beans to count in his household.

But he has found many piles of paper.

Jeeves discovered that these piles make up a paper trail.

He wonders why it's called a paper trail.

When Jeeves last created a trail on paper, he was a puppy.

Jeeves has heard of trail mix.

Trail mix is a snack food consisting of many things like nuts, raisins and sometimes chocolate.

Like all dogs, Jeeves can't eat raisins or chocolate.

They can cause death.

Jeeves doesn't know why anyone would create a paper trail to take to the accountant.

Between his house and the accountant's office, there are plenty of paved roads.

There's even a nature trail.

But there's no paper trail.

Thankfully, there's no trail mix.

Jeeves set off to find answers to these perplexing questions.

He began to understand the anxiety that tax season brings.

Jeeves learned that "bean counter" is a disparaging term for accountants. Ironically, he knows one accountant who refers to himself in this way. He even offers jelly beans to his clients.

According to phrases.org, the term dates back to 1907.

The earliest reference to the use of bean counter in connection with accountants occurred in a 1919 edition of Fort Wayne's *News-Sentinel*.

In 1975, *Forbes Magazine* referred to a "smart, tightfisted and austere bean counter accountant from rural Kentucky" (word-detective.com).

After more than 100 years, bean counter has become part of the vernacular.

Jeeves discovered that the term paper trail has a more recent history.

According to merriam-webster.com, the first known use of the phrase occurred in 1955.

Merriam-Webster also defines paper trail as "documents (as financial records) from which a person's actions may be traced or opinions learned."

Jeeves is happy that we have bean counters to reduce anxiety during tax season.

But he will always refer to them as accountants.

After all, Jeeves knows that they went to school and passed examinations to earn their professional designation as CPA's.

In his opinion, they should receive recognition for their efforts.

Jeeves is also happy that paper trail means documents or financial records.

He couldn't imagine anyone wanting to look at his paper trail.

That would be taxing in any season.

🐾 TIMES ARE CHANGIN'...

Jeeves has seen television commercials about the new watch from Apple.

Over a million watches have been ordered.

They're supposed to come out by June.

According to Apple's website, the watch is designed to "let you do familiar things more quickly and conveniently."

Jeeves doesn't pay much attention to time.

He knows when it's about 6:00 a.m.

That's when his stomach tells him that it's time for breakfast.

He also knows when it's about 4:00 p.m.

That's when his stomach tells him that it's time for dinner.

Apart from those two stomach driven events, Jeeves has no timetable.

So, he doesn't need an Apple or any other type of watch.

He wonders why so many are preoccupied with time.

And, he wonders why so many are preoccupied with saving time.

Jeeves was surprised to learn that, last fall, Major League Baseball tested new experimental rules.

These rules were developed to improve the pace of baseball and reduce how much time it takes to complete a game.

Until last fall's trial, baseball games lasted until they were over.

Baseball has always been a game with no clock.

When Jeeves watches baseball, he expects at least nine innings of play, or more.

He doesn't expect this familiar sport to run more quickly or conveniently.

Jeeves doesn't know if the experimental rules will take hold.

But, he does know that baseball will not be the same, for him, if these rules do take hold.

During its meeting of April 14, 2015, Lincoln City Council was asked to consider a time saving measure (Item 9 C).

Specifically, Councilmen heard a presentation from City Attorney Jonathan Hobbs regarding Procedural Rules for City Council Meetings under Ordinance No. 898B.

If this ordinance is repealed and reenacted, public comments may be limited to three minutes per person.

Currently, the ordinance limits public comments to five minutes per person.

Jeeves wondered how much time neighboring cities allow for comments.

So, he checked.

Jeeves found that City of Rocklin allows five minutes per person.

And, he found that the cities of Colfax, Folsom and Roseville allow three minutes per person.

City of Roseville also limits the total time for citizens addressing council to 25 minutes.

Jeeves also found that the cities of Loomis and Auburn have different approaches.

City of Loomis allows three to five minutes per person.

The city's mayor determines the length of time based on a few factors including the number of people who wish to speak, the agenda item and/or the issue.

City of Auburn is flexible.

According to the city clerk, Auburn has no set time for citizens who address council.

Jeeves doesn't know how much meeting time City of Lincoln will save if it limits citizens who address council to three minutes from five minutes.

But, he does know that four citizens stood up on April 14 to address this proposed change.

Three citizens indicated that they would prefer that the time limit remain at five minutes.

A fourth citizen indicated that he would prefer that the time limit be three minutes with an opportunity for an extension to five minutes.

Unlike them, Jeeves doesn't care about how much time allotted to citizens who wish to address city council.

What he does care about is the equitable treatment of each citizen who takes time to attend and address city council.

Jeeves shook his head when he heard Councilman Gabriel Hydrick offer his comments following the city attorney's presentation on this issue.

Councilmen Hydrick indicated he likes to hear people out.

And, Councilman Hydrick went on to comment that when he was Mayor, he often extended time to citizens who addressed council.

Jeeves has been watching Lincoln city council meetings since he was a pup.

And, he can confirm that Hydrick, as mayor, did extend time from time to time.

But, based on his observations, Jeeves believes that Hydrick extended time if he liked what he was hearing.

When the issues were contentious and he didn't like what he was hearing, Hydrick limited comments to five minutes.

He granted no extensions.

Hydrick is not an exception.

Based on Jeeves' observations, Mayor Paul Joiner has shown the same tendency as evidenced by his behavior during the April 14 meeting.

A citizen addressed council about the proposed ordinance time change.

His comments were contentious.

Mayor Joiner limited his comments to five minutes.

He granted no extension.

Yet, during Item 5 of the meeting under Presentations (Item 5 of the Agenda), both Mayor Joiner and Councilman Hydrick were active participants concerning an upcoming event at Lincoln's airport.

That discussion lasted almost nine minutes.

Mayor Joiner went so far as to comment about the aircraft structure and purchasing additional tickets for his family members.

Councilman Hydrick went so far as to offer comments about promoting the event at another airport and weighed-in on the event poster.

In Jeeves' opinion, they were actively engaged because they liked what they were hearing.

Jeeves believes that there's nothing wrong with the mayor granting more time for an issue he likes.

But, Jeeves also believes there's something wrong when the mayor fails to allot the same amount for an issue he dislikes.

For the record, Jeeves realizes that there are no time limitations placed on citizens who appear to make presentations versus the limitations on those citizens who appear to address council.

Maybe there should be the same time limitations on all citizens no matter when they appear on the city council meeting agenda.

Regardless, Jeeves hopes that, whatever ordinance Lincoln city council reenacts, the mayor applies both time limitations and any extensions equitably.

And, if Lincoln's mayor needs a watch to help him keep time, Jeeves believes that he could be one in a million if he orders his watch from Apple.

They're supposed to come out by June.

🐾 TOUGH ENOUGH...

Jeeves knows that this year is an election year.

And he knows that Lincoln voters will have the opportunity to choose three city Councilmen.

Jeeves doesn't know if our incumbent Councilmen will seek re-election.

Nor does he know how many others may compete.

But he applauds all men and women who seek leadership positions.

Based on all that he observed over the past few months, Jeeves knows that election campaigns can be tough to mount and even tougher to fight.

After a city election is over, Jeeves wondered what it's like to serve as a Councilman.

In particular, he wondered how much time it takes.

Jeeves tries to watch every City Council meeting - usually two per month.

They are scheduled to start at 6 p.m.

Before each meeting, Jeeves downloads the agenda from the city's website and prints it.

He likes to follow along.

Jeeves does not print the attachments.

They can consist of hundreds of pages.

Some meetings are short and some meetings are long.

Many extend beyond Jeeves' 10:30 p.m. bedtime.

Besides these meetings, Jeeves wondered how many more hours per week each Councilman can expect to devote to the city's business.

So he consulted several former city Councilmen.

Jeeves was surprised by what he learned.

Former city Councilman Donnie Baxter told him that, on average, he devoted 40 hours per week

Baxter also told Jeeves that more complex city council issues demanded more of his time.

Former city Councilman, Michael Storz told him that he devoted a minimum of 20 to 25 hours per week.

Depending on the issues, he regularly spent more time.

Storz told Jeeves that "it's like having another full-time job."

Former city Councilman Charles Kellar also devoted a minimum of 20 to 30 hours per week during his two terms of office from 1984 until 1992.

While he served as Mayor of Lincoln, he also served as Chairman of Roseville Hospital Board.

Kellar told Jeeves that "when people asked him what he did for recreation, he told them that he attended committee meetings."

Former city Councilman Ron Barringer echoed Baxter, Storz and Kellar.

In addition to devoting many hours in Lincoln, sometimes he traveled to other cities such as Washington D.C., San Diego and Los Angeles in order to further the city's business.

All of these activities took time away from his family and from his business.

Barringer explained to Jeeves that although his term of office "cost a lot in business, it was a way of giving back to this great city."

Jeeves learned a lot from these former city Councilmen.

He learned that city council requires far more time than attendance at two meetings a month.

Jeeves also learned that time spent on the city's business means time away from family, friends, recreation and other responsibilities such as earning a living.

These four men, like others before and after them, sacrificed their time in order to make Lincoln a better city.

At one time, each ran for city council.

Jeeves doesn't know if their campaigns were tough to mount or to tough to fight.

But he does know that they were tough enough to serve.

Jeeves hopes those who seek to serve in the future are tough enough too.

🐾 A LONG LIFE SHORT-LIVED...

Jeeves is a little dog at the end of a short leash.
This week, he celebrates his seventh birthday.
In dog years, that's middle-aged.
Jeeves doesn't feel middle-aged.
He feels like a teenager.
He can still run faster than any animal his size, even squirrels.
And, he has the appetite of a young boy.
Jeeves looks forward to a long life.
He should last another seven years, or more.
After all, his handlers ensure that he has a proper diet.
They also ensure that he receives plenty of exercise.
And, they do their best to keep him safe.
Sometimes it isn't easy for them to keep Jeeves free from harm.
Alas, in Jeeves' neighborhood, other handlers are not as careful with their dogs.
Cindy, his poodle girlfriend, has noticed it too.
Some handlers walk their dogs on long leashes instead of short leashes.
Of course, long leashes are attractive to dogs.
They offer greater freedom for them to roam and sniff when out for their walks.
But, when these dogs encounter other dogs, like Jeeves and Cindy, danger looms.
Dog handlers believe that their dogs are friendly.
Jeeves and Cindy believe that they are friendly too.
But, from time to time, their patience is tried especially by dogs on long leashes.
When this happens, they growl and become unfriendly.
They wish it didn't happen.
Neither Jeeves nor Cindy has any idea what overcomes them.
Their bad behavior frightens them.
Sometimes, Jeeves behaves like a junkyard dog.
Then, he's prepared to take on any dog no matter how large.
Other times, Jeeves behaves like a possum.
Then, he curls up and tries to hide.
Sometimes, Cindy behaves like a lioness.

Then, she's fierce as she protects her pride.

Other, times, Cindy behaves like a princess.

Then, she's ready to hold court.

Neither Jeeves nor Cindy claims to be perfect day in and day out.

Like all dogs, they aren't friendly 100 percent of the time.

And, they challenge any dog handler who claims otherwise.

Jeeves and Cindy don't know what to do about handlers who fail to shorten the leashes of their dogs when they encounter other dogs.

Jeeves and Cindy do know how quickly any dog's behavior can change.

They know that a growl can manifest into a bite.

Jeeves and Cindy would never set out to bite another dog.

Nor would they expect another dog to bite them.

Yet, they know it happens.

And, when it happens, a dog that inflicts a bite risks an unspeakable fate.

It's a fate that might make a dog's long leash obsolete.

Jeeves looks forward to another seven years.

He plans to enjoy them from the end of his short leash.

🐾 HAPPINESS IS...

Last week, Jeeves read Columbia University's *Earth Institute First World Happiness Report*.

United Nations Conference on Happiness commissioned this report.

Jeeves discussed the report with the dogs.

The dogs focused on Figure 2.5 which shows "Average Life Satisfaction by Country."

Luna is part German Shepherd.

She was surprised to discover that Germany ranks 22 on this list.

Cindy is a French Poodle .

She was surprised to discover that France ranks 34 on this list.

Nasha is a Scottie.

She was surprised to discover that Scotland, as part of the United Kingdom, ranks 24 on this list.

Buster is a Shih Tzu.

He was surprised to discover that China doesn't even appear on this list.

And all the dogs were surprised to discover that the United States ranks 10 on this list.

Costa Rica ranks first, Denmark ranks second, Ireland ranks third, Norway ranks fourth and Finland ranks fifth.

Jeeves wondered why these countries rank higher than the United States.

Our Declaration of Independence includes the inalienable right to the pursuit of happiness.

Jeeves also wondered if pets played any role in the *World Happiness Report*.

If so, he wondered if Costa Rica has a dog breed that makes people happier.

Jeeves conducted his own research via the Internet.

He could find no particular dog associated with this country.

But he found that the proportion of Costa Rican households that keep dogs is 3.6 higher than households that keep cats (Society & Animals 9:2 2001)

Jeeves also found that 24 per cents of households keep wild animals as pets with parrots being most common.

Alas, Jeeves found no mention of pets in the *World Happiness Report*.

Instead, he learned that the happiest countries tend to be high income countries that also have high degrees of social equality, trust and quality of governance.

The United States is a high income country.

But despite increases in our living standards over the last half century, Jeeves learned that the "U.S. has experienced no rise in life satisfaction."

During this period, "inequality has soared, social trust has declined, and the public has lost faith in government."

While levels of trust fell in this country, trust rose in countries like Denmark.

The report also shows that "richer people are happier than poorer people, but over time the society did not become happier as it became richer."

Jeeves also learned that mental health is important to happiness.

Yet, only a "quarter of people with mental illness are in treatment, compared with well over three quarters for most physical conditions."

And Jeeves learned that married people tend to be happier than single people and a stable family life contributes to happiness.

Jeeves will continue to mull over the report's 158 pages.

He's happy to be part of a stable home.

Although Jeeves learned that he find greater happiness through marriage, he has no plans to walk down the aisle.

Overall, he's a happy little dog at the end of his short leash.

And he's happy with the "happiness" findings except for how our country ranks.

On Jeeves' list, the U.S. will always come first.

🐾 IF ONLY...

Jeeves is excited about the upcoming Voices of Lincoln Poetry Contest.

This contest is open to everyone.

Over the past 10 years, the poetry contest has attracted hundreds of entries from around the world.

This year, the contest invites poets to enter under five categories including "Only in America," "Happy Endings," "Strange But True" and "Unforgettable."

The fifth contest category perplexes Jeeves.

It's called "If Pets Could Talk."

Jeeves wondered why there's an "if" associated with this category.

Pets always have plenty to convey - no "ifs" about it.

Jeeves and the Downtown Dogs communicate regularly around the fountain in Beermann Plaza.

And, his neighborhood friends, Cindy, Molly, Nasha and Billy engage in lively exchanges while they check their pee-mails around the fire hydrants in Lincoln Hills.

Billy, in particular, makes them laugh.

Jeeves doesn't know if comedy is a springer spaniel trait or if it's a Billy trait.

Regardless, their spaniel friend always gives the neighborhood dogs a chuckle.

Jeeves continued to wonder why Poets Club of Lincoln came up with "If Pets Could Talk" as a category.

So, he traveled to Land Park Zoo to seek professional advice from other animals.

Jeeves consulted with the owls.

After all, they're supposed to be wise.

The owls explained to Jeeves that animals do not talk.

They don't need to speak.

Animals express themselves in other ways.

Unlike humans who speak many languages, animals communicate differently.

And, the animal language is a universal one.

It's based on other communication skills rather than speech.

These skills allow each animal to understand all the other animals.

For example, the tortoise and the giraffe will stick their necks out on any issue.

But, if challenged, the tortoise will retreat into his shell.

On the other hand, the giraffe will always stand tall.

Zebras tend to see the world in black and white.

While cows may seem vacuous, it's only because they like to chew things over and over.

Pigs have two expressions.

Depending how they feel when they wake up, they will either snort or oink.

Apes are playful.

They like to mimic those around them.

Snakes can be venomous.

So, other animals, except mongooses, stay clear.

Mongooses like snakes, particularly cobras.

Lions, leopards and all the other cats are naturally inquisitive.

Sometimes, this trait can be detrimental to their well-being.

The owls reminded Jeeves that curiosity killed a cat.

All animals communicate, in some way, to get along.

Some communicate by making gestures, some communicate by making noises and some communicate by doing both simultaneously.

None say a word.

So, animals have to pay attention to understand what other animals are trying to convey.

Jeeves wondered if the animals in the zoo get along so well because they separated by fences.

He reminded the owls about the poem by Robert Frost called *Mending Wall*.

Frost wrote that "Good fences make good neighbors."

The owls reminded Jeeves that, even in the wild, animals still get along.

Consider Walt Disney Studios' new Disney nature production called *Monkey Kingdom*.

For 120 minutes, real monkeys act out their lives in their natural habitat without fences.

They have no script.

So, no monkey speaks.

Yet, movie audiences are treated to a plot, a love story, a heroine, a hero, villains, and even a chase scene.

Like all wild animals, the monkeys persist despite their enemies.

And, they deliver a story that's worthy of Walt Disney Studios.

Jeeves expressed his thanks to the owls for their insights.

He now understands the difference between communicating and talking.

Jeeves looks forward to reading the results of the Voices of Lincoln Poetry Contest, especially entries in "If Pets Could Talk" category.

He hopes another poet like Robert Frost emerges.

And next year, he hopes the poetry contest includes a category called "If Humans Could Communicate Like Pets."

Meanwhile, Jeeves can hardly wait to hear what his pet friends, like Cindy, Molly, Nasha and Billy, would say if only they could talk.

🐾 ENCHANTING...

Jeeves loves Beermann Plaza.

For him, it's a special place.

Like Jeeves, the Downtown Dogs love it too.

They also like to sit by the fountain.

Sometimes, if there's a breeze, they catch the fountain spray.

On a hot August day, even a few drops of water are refreshing.

Others also find Beermann Plaza special.

Jeeves has seen children toss coins in the fountain while they make wishes.

He hopes that all their wishes come true.

Jeeves has seen others eat their lunch in Beermann Plaza.

They sit at any one of the three fixed metal tables.

And, Jeeves has seen others take time out to sit on any one of the plaza's seven benches.

Some sit and seem to enjoy their own thoughts while others seem to enjoy books.

Thursday, he saw two men stretched out on two different benches.

He assumes they enjoyed afternoon siestas.

Occasionally, Jeeves will see "plein air" painters set up their easels in the plaza.

He hopes that they find Beermann Plaza as inspiring as he does.

Jeeves also knows of couples who held their wedding receptions in the plaza.

And, he knows of others who held different types of celebrations like anniversaries and birthdays.

Like Jeeves, they treasure Beermann Plaza.

They reserve it for important events in their lives.

So, they treat it carefully like any prized possession.

Jeeves recently heard about an event that took place in Beermann Plaza.

The event involved a young couple.

The young couple are high school students.

They went on a date.

The date was held by the fountain in Beermann Plaza.

It wasn't just any date.

It was their first date.

And, it was a dinner date.

Before the date took place, the young man set-up a table and two chairs in front of the fountain.

He laid out a tablecloth and place settings for himself and his date.

Then, he brought his date to the plaza where he presented her with flowers.

His father, who he enlisted to help, brought and served them dinner.

Someone, who saw the evening unfold, described it as "enchanting."

Jeeves wishes he could have seen it too.

He admires the young man for coming up with the idea, making arrangements and treating his date to a wonderful evening.

Jeeves hopes that this young couple will have happy memories of their first date.

If so, those memories will always be associated with Beermann Plaza.

Except for one sign that says "No Skateboarding," there are no other signs in Beermann Plaza with other rules and regulations.

Jeeves hopes that no more signs are ever needed.

He believes that most everyone treasures Beermann Plaza.

Yet, he knows others view it differently.

They see it as simply a place for a band and vendors during the summers' weekly Farmers' Market.

And, they see it simply as place for a bounce house during the monthly Food Mob event.

Jeeves believes that there's room for them too.

But, he wishes that they viewed Beermann Plaza as a treasure rather than an adjunct to their event.

If they did, they would leave it as they found it.

They would leave it clean.

They would wash away the spills that mark the tables, the benches and the walkways.

Jeeves believes that it's not enough to just pick up the litter.

Others, who may want to go on a first date, hold a wedding reception or make a wish, should find the plaza as it should be - not only clean but enchanting.

After all, Beermann Plaza is a special place.

Jeeves believes it deserves special care.

🐾 BACK OF THE PACK...

Jeeves tries to learn something new everyday.

He doesn't always succeed.

Some days, Jeeves discovers how much more he needs to learn.

Last Monday was such a day.

Jeeves went for his usual midday walk in Downtown Lincoln.

He checked each of the two water hydrants on Lincoln Boulevard and F Street for any "pee-mails" from the Downtown Dogs.

Finding no new messages, Jeeves proceeded along Fifth Street.

He came across a sandwich sign in front of Umpqua Bank.

Jeeves doesn't know why they're called sandwich signs.

He's never found a sandwich hanging on any sign.

Nor has he found a whiff of ham or cheese on any sign.

But, Jeeves did find a notice that intrigued him.

The notice was an appeal to "Help Our Kids Back to School" as part of this year's "Backpack4Kids Drive."

So, he decided to sit and read the notice in its entirety.

Jeeves learned that many students, from kindergarten through fifth grade, need school supplies as well as backpacks.

When Jeeves telephoned Western Placer Unified School District, he also learned that Lincoln has 7 elementary schools.

And, he leaned that more than 3,000 children attend those schools.

Jeeves was surprised to discover that as many as 10% of these students need supplies because of their family financial circumstances.

If so, 300 students need help.

With appropriate and adequate supplies, Jeeves believes that students can accomplish much more than without them.

Jeeves wondered what he could do to help.

He learned that kindergarten students need boxes of Crayola Crayons in 8 primary colors while second and third grade students need Crayola Crayons in 16 colors.

Other students need erasers, glue sticks, No. 2 Ticonderoga pencils, 3" by 5" index cards and much more.

The list is long.

Jeeves bought crayons, pencils, pencil crayons and a back pack.

He dropped them in the box at Umpqua Bank, 571 5th Street.

While there, Jeeves also admired the new art show by Lincoln Hills Painters Club.

He hopes that you will stop by and admire it too.

Jeeves thanks the sponsors of this year's "Backpack4KidsDrive."

He hopes others will thank them too.

The sponsors are Gulfstream, Kiwanis Club of Lincoln, Soroptimist International of Lincoln and SCHOOLS (Sun City Helping Our Outstanding Lincoln Schools).

Like Umpqua Bank, other businesses and organizations are showing their support by offering drop-off boxes for supplies.

Drop-off boxes can also be found at WalMart (255 Lincoln Boulevard), Sun City Lincoln Hills Kilaga Springs Lodge (1167 Sun City Boulevard), Sun City Lincoln Hills Orchard Creek Lodge (965 Orchard Creek Lane) and Pink Box Donut Shop (820 Sterling Parkway).

This month, elementary, middle and high school students return to school.

Jeeves wishes he could attend with them.

He knows that he has a lot to learn.

Jeeves would like to start school this week.

So, he bought himself a backpack.

In a classroom, along with other students, Jeeves knows that he could learn something new everyday.

He would sit at the front of the class.

Jeeves wouldn't want to miss anything.

Alas, he discovered that dogs can't attend Lincoln schools.

So, Jeeves will have to be content helping other students.

He has donated his new backpack.

But, Jeeves won't give up his quest to find a sandwich hanging from a board.

🐾 WEIGHTY MATTERS...

Jeeves enjoyed his break.

While his family members were traveling, Jeeves stayed home

He caught up with friends and family members.

After spending time with his French poodle friend Cindy, Jeeves exchanged telephone calls with his cousin Poppy.

Poppy is part Labrador and part Great Pyrenees.

She is lovingly referred to as either Labrenees or Great Pyrador.

At 85 pounds, Poppy is 12 times heavier than Jeeves.

So, when Poppy weighs-in, Jeeves pays attention.

Poppy lives in Manchester Center, Vermont.

She explained to Jeeves that Manchester Center is part of Manchester.

And, Poppy believes that Manchester is the best town in the world.

Jeeves wondered what makes Manchester so special to Poppy.

The 2010 census reveals that 2,120 people live in Manchester Center out of a total population of 4,391 that live in Manchester.

How could a town with less than 5,000 people be better than a city, like Lincoln, that has more than 44,000 people?

Poppy directed Jeeves to the Internet and suggested that he look up Manchester on TripAdvisor.com.

Jeeves looked and was surprised by what he found.

Manchester offers 15 hotels, 17 vacation rentals, 62 restaurants and 30 things to do.

Poppy told Jeeves that Manchester will soon have another luxury hotel.

It's due to open this fall and will be called The Kimpton Taconic Hotel.

And, Manchester has an outlet mall too

Jeeves wondered how Manchester could attract a Kimpton Hotel and an outlet mall when Lincoln couldn't keep Staples.

"Didn't the downtown stores object when the mall opened?" Jeeves asked.

And, Jeeves wondered how could long-standing retail stores compete with discount stores.

Poppy explained that Manchester approached the concept of an outlet mall differently.

Instead of building a separate mall that would draw customers away from Manchester Center, it broke up the mall.

The outlet mall stores were strategically placed.

Either a new store occupied an empty building next to an existing downtown retail store or it occupied a new building constructed on vacant downtown property.

"As a result," Poppy said "you may find each of the more than 40 outlet stores, such as Armani or The Gap, housed next to jewelry or book stores, such as McWayne Jewelers or Northshire Bookstore, that have been doing business in Manchester Center for many years."

And, the exterior of each outlet store was architecturally designed so that its facade blends in with other existing store fronts.

The outlet mall stores look like New England buildings that have been around for a long time.

"As far as I can tell cousin Jeeves," Poppy remarked, "what distinguishes an outlet mall store from an independent store is simply a small sign in the window."

Poppy went on to explain that everyone benefited from this approach.

"The downtown not only retained its historic downtown and preserved its charm but offered customers more choices and became a tourist venue - all at the same time."

"Plus, as customers walk from store to store, they have a chance to see and enjoy the city's many other attractive features."

"So," Poppy offered "if Lincoln wants to attract hotels and visitors while it preserves its historic downtown, perhaps it could obtain and position a mall in the same way as Manchester."

"A mall doesn't have to compete with a city's downtown retail stores."

"Instead, it can complement an existing downtown infrastructure if it's subdivided into separate entities."

Jeeves liked this idea.

But, he couldn't believe that an outlet mall would be enough to attract so many hotels, inns and restaurants.

"A town must offer more than just 40 new places to shop in order to create demand for so many hotels and inns!" Jeeves declared.

Poppy explained that Manchester more than a shopping venue, it's also a gateway.

During the winter, Manchester is a gateway for skiing.

While Manchester may have no ski hills, Bromley and Stratton ski resorts can be found within a short driving distance.

During the fall, Manchester is a gateway for viewing the changes in tree colors.

And, during other seasons, Manchester is a gateway for hiking, fishing, golfing, cycling and other sporting activities.

For example, it's estimated that the recent Vermont Summer Festival Horse Show brought in more than 20 million tourist dollars to Manchester and it surrounding towns and villages.

Poppy also reminded Jeeves that Vermont is famous for maple syrup.

People come to Manchester to buy syrup too.

"Is Lincoln a gateway for anything?" Poppy asked Jeeves.

"Funny you should ask," Jeeves said.

"Last week, I read an interesting column in our local weekly newspaper."*

Richard Pearl wrote the column.

Mr. Pearl is Chairman of City of Lincoln's Economic Development Committee.

From Mr. Pearl's report, we learned that *"there is a substantial opportunity to capitalize on area and regional agriculture by branding Lincoln as a "gateway" to Placer County and Sierra foothills agricultural industries."*

Mr. Pearl also went on to write *"we're already a hot-bed of agriculture. In 2014, for example, visitors spent $980 million on agri-tourism in Placer County, representing $27 million dollars in local tax revenue and supporting nearly 11,000 jobs."*

"That's wonderful news!" remarked Poppy.

Jeeves agreed.

Both he and Poppy look forward to reading more economic development committee reports from Mr. Pearl.

Poppy remarked "maybe City of Lincoln, like Manchester, will find additional gateways to success."

And, she went on to say "it wasn't easy for Manchester and it won't be easy for Lincoln."

"No change happens in any town or city without some resistance and controversy."

"For example, despite the fact our new library was built by private funds, we heard plenty from naysayers and dissenters - some of whom were our elected officials."

"A new library built with private funds!" exclaimed Jeeves.

"Yep," said Poppy "I'll tell you more about it next week."

"Manchester residents don't rely on their elected officials to get things done and Lincoln residents shouldn't either."

"Meanwhile, Jeeves, I hope that you enjoyed your break."

"But, it's time for you to get back to work," growled Poppy.

"I've missed your weekly blog."

When Poppy weighs-in, Jeeves pays attention.

After all, she's 12 times heavier than Jeeves.

* *Lincoln News Messenger,* August 6, 2015, Page A4, "Economic Development Committee plans strategic initiatives."

🐾 THE SNIFF TEST...

Jeeves misses the Carnegie Library.

He also misses the smell of its books.

Nothing pleased Jeeves more than walking into Lincoln's downtown library and getting a whiff of its books.

From a book Jeeves borrowed from the Carnegie Library, he discovered that books smell because of the chemicals used to make their paper, ink and binding.

Jeeves wishes that he could relive those Carnegie Library smells.

Alas, his favorite library closed June 29, 2011.

Jeeves wonders what it will take to reopen Carnegie Library.

He recalled his telephone conversation with his cousin Poppy, the Great Pyrador, about her local library in Manchester, Vermont.

Poppy is part Labrador and part Great Pyrenees.

Last week, Poppy mentioned to Jeeves that Manchester built a new library with private funds.

Jeeves was amazed.

He wondered how a town of 4,400 people could come up with enough money to fund a $5.4 million project.

And, he wondered if Lincoln could come up with enough money to reopen the Carnegie Library.

So, Jeeves called Poppy at her home in Vermont.

She directed Jeeves to the Manchester Community Library website (http://mclvt.org/).

"Upload and read the brochure called *Case Statement*," Poppy said.

Jeeves was excited to read the subtitle on the brochure, 'Building Our Gateway to the World.'

As recently reported in our local weekly newspaper and in last week's blog, City of Lincoln's Economic Development Committee wants to build a "gateway to Placer County and Sierra foothills agricultural industries."

Jeeves wondered if economic development could set its sights higher than Placer County or the Sierra Foothills.

Why not build a gateway to the world like Manchester Community Library?

And, if not the world, why not build a gateway to downtown Lincoln by reopening Carnegie Library?

If Manchester can open a new library, why can't Lincoln reopen an old one?

Jeeves asked Poppy if she had any answers to his questions.

Poppy explained that although the Manchester Community Library is primarily funded through private donations, the library does seek funds from its local government to help cover staffing costs.

Manchester Community Library operating budget for the 2014-2015 year was about $468,000.

Even with its local government's full support of $198,000, the library still needs about $270,000 more in private contributions to meet its operating expenses.

Poppy wondered how Lincoln's libraries are funded.

Jeeves directed her to City of Lincoln's website (www.ci.lincoln.ca.us) where she could find the city's budget for 2015-2016.

Poppy read City of Lincoln's budget and found that $512,492 has been allocated to the library's 2015-2016 operations.

She was surprised to discover that Lincoln's library operates on just $44,492 more than Manchester's library.

Lincoln is a city of 44,000 residents while Manchester is a town of 4,400 residents.

"For a city of Lincoln's size, that's not much money compared to a town of Manchester's size!" Poppy exclaimed.

She wondered how much Lincoln residents donate to help run its libraries.

Jeeves advised Poppy that Friends of Lincoln Library donated about $95,000 in 2014 to support programs like Mother Goose on the Loose.

"That's wonderful" observed Poppy "but, that's still $170,000 less than Manchester residents donated."

"Do the math Jeeves, she said "and you will find that the average annual Lincoln donation is about $2.16 per resident whereas the average annual Manchester donation is $61.36 per resident and that's before they make their donations to the capital fund."

Based on Poppy's understanding, Lincoln's way of library funding is opposite to Manchester's way of library funding.

In Manchester, residents contribute more funds than its local government.

"As you now know," said Poppy "Manchester believes that our library is a gateway to the world - what does Lincoln believe about its Carnegie Library?"

She continued by saying "if Lincoln residents value their Carnegie Library, perhaps they need to think of new ways to re-purpose and fund it."

Instead of being a place for book borrowing, Poppy wondered if the Carnegie could be a gateway for other things.

Perhaps the Carnegie could be a gateway for technology where members gain access to downloadable audio books and e-books that are compatible with a variety of MP3 devices.

Poppy explained that Manchester Community Library is also a hub for technology help with free computer training, online tutorials and digital services a well as access to laptop bars, computer work tables, Wi-Fi and licensed databases.

And, perhaps the Carnegie could be a gateway for meetings through the rental of multi-use meeting rooms or private study rooms to students, tutors, business people and community groups.

Poppy also explained that Manchester Community Library's 'touch down work spaces' are an asset to business people who need a place to work away from home or while they're in town to meet clients.

These work spaces rent for $10 for the first two hours and $10 per hour thereafter.

Conference space is available for $20 per hour with a two-hour minimum.

All fees are lower for library members.

Rental fees are just one of many ways that Manchester Community Library has found to generate additional monies to cover expenses.

Poppy wondered if Lincoln libraries could find new opportunities to generate new revenue and reopen the Carnegie Library.

For example, perhaps it could charge non resident and business membership fees.

While Manchester doesn't charge residents a membership fee, it does charge nonresidents a $45 annual membership fee.

"I value my library membership and view it as a privilege not as a right," declared Poppy "so, like other Manchester residents, I am prepared to dig deep and donate more for that privilege."

"Your Carnegie library doesn't have to be a gateway to the world," said Poppy "but I believe it could can so much more than a sign that says 'Closed'."

She went on to say, "if your city government is prepared to set aside more than a half-million dollars for services, it shows some level of commitment to your libraries."

Poppy wondered if Lincoln residents, besides Friends of Lincoln Library, are willing to show their level of commitment.

If so, are residents prepared to make an annual donation of more than $2.16 per person?

If not, are residents willing to come up with other ways to fund your libraries?

"These are always tough questions for residents of any town or city to answer," remarked Poppy.

She lamented "Jeeves, while you like the smell of books, please remember that many more prefer the smell of money which may not bode well for your Carnegie Library."

🐾 INTRANSIENT...

Jeeves discovered 4 or 5 new people in Downtown Lincoln.

They showed up recently.

Like Jeeves, they spend a lot of time in downtown Lincoln.

They came with bedrolls, backpacks and many other things attached to them.

Jeeves believes that they are tourists.

And, Jeeves was so excited about the arrival of these men that he called a meeting of the Downtown Dogs.

Alas, the dogs did not share his excitement.

Instead, the Downtown Dogs wondered how Jeeves could believe that these men are tourists.

"They're transients!" said the dogs.

Jeeves begged to disagree.

He reminded the dogs that Lincoln now has a monthly Food Truck Mob event which has been designed by Downtown Lincoln Association to attract thousands of people to downtown even if it interferes with surrounding businesses.

"Don't you believe that this downtown association event has made this city a diner's delight?" Jeeves asked. "It should be no surprise to anyone that these men came to downtown Lincoln."

The dogs wondered how Jeeves could continue to believe that these men are tourists.

"They're transients" the dogs repeated. "That's why they carry sleeping bags and all their worldly belongings with them."

Once again, Jeeves begged to disagree.

He reminded the dogs that last Friday, during a special meeting, Lincoln City Council voted to support the resolution to participate in Roseville's Business Improvement District/Placer Valley Sports Complex and Tourism Marketing District.

"As a result," Jeeves said "I'm sure that Lincoln's hotels are already full. If they want to sleep, these men have no choice but to carry their own beds."

The dogs wondered how Jeeves could continue to believe that these men are tourists.

"Have you looked at them?" the dogs asked. "They are unshaven and they smell because they don't shower. That means they're transients."

And, once again, Jeeves begged to disagree.

He reminded the dogs that people are not always as they seem.

"Just because they are unshaven and they smell doesn't mean they're transients. I believe that it means that they're too busy to shave and shower," said Jeeves. "So, they must be important men."

The dogs were exasperated by Jeeves.

"Jeeves! Jeeves! Jeeves!" the dogs remonstrated "they spend their time wandering up and down downtown Lincoln's alleys. How can you say they're important? They're transients!"

And, once again, Jeeves begged to disagree.

He reminded the dogs that Lincoln's Economic Development Committee has hired consultants, bought new software programs and spent many thousands of dollars on ways to attract new investors and businesses to Lincoln.

Even if Downtown Lincoln Association and Economic Development Committee can't get Lincoln to come to Lincoln, at least they've succeeded in getting at 4 or 5 new investors to come to Lincoln.

"You may call them transients, but I call them savvy businessmen" said Jeeves. "Just as you shouldn't judge a book by its cover, these men know that they shouldn't judge a building by its facade. I believe that these men are looking at downtown buildings from all angles. They want to make sound real estate investments."

The dogs were vexed by Jeeves.

"We have seen these men looking in garbage cans," shouted the dogs. "These men are not looking for properties, they're looking for food. They're transients!"

And, once again, Jeeves begged to disagree.

He reminded the dogs that you can tell a lot about a city by looking at its garbage.

"When these men look in our garbage cans, they won't find a Taco Bell wrapper nor will they find leftovers from Mimi's, Applebee's, Beermann's, Chilli's, Panera Bread. or Wendy's" said Jeeves. "Our garbage is devoid of chain restaurant residue. Instead, they will find that our garbage rivals cities like Beverly Hills and Martha's Vineyard. Ironically, what these men don't find in our garbage will tell them what Lincoln really has to offer."

The dogs were apoplectic over Jeeves.

"Jeeves, how many more times are we going to have to tell you that they're not investors?" said the dogs emphatically. "All they do is sit on the benches in Beermann Plaza and in front and behind the Carnegie Library. They're transients."

And, once again, Jeeves begged to disagree.

He reminded the dogs that these men are important people.

While the dogs may perceive these men as being idle, in all probability, they are reviewing the pros and cons of their prospective Lincoln investments.

Their kind of analyses takes time.

"As I've stated before, they are busy men," said Jeeves. They are investors. And, I believe that they are so important their brokers come to them not the other way around."

"For the eighth time," the dogs said "they are not important, they're transients."

And, once again, Jeeves begged to disagree.

He reminded the dogs that many investors and many important people behave outside the norm.

They can be eccentric like Minerology Owner Clive Palmer or IKEA Founder Ingvar Kamprad who rank first and second, respectively, on the list of 10 most Eccentric Millionaires and Billionaires (listverse.com).

"And, let's not forget Howard Hughes who ranks fifth on the list," said Jeeves. "In the later years of his life, he wasn't known for his hygiene nor for his manner of dress - both were poor despite his wealth."

The dogs were now totally fed up with Jeeves.

"For the last time," the dogs pleaded "they are not tourists, they're not investors and they're not important. Next you'll be telling us that they have corporate jets parked at Lincoln Airport. They're transients!"

Although Jeeves didn't know if they owned corporate jets, he told the dogs that he could prove these men were important.

Just like the President of the United States of America who receives a police escort whenever and where ever he travels, Jeeves saw one of these men receive a police escort.

Two police cars showed up in front of the Carnegie Library on Saturday, August 9.

Not only did Lincoln police put this man in a cruiser, they also loaded his bed roll plus all his belongings in the trunk of their vehicle.

Maybe the police took him to Lincoln's airport.

Jeeves doesn't know.

What he does know is that Lincoln's finest took time to recognize at least one of these men as important even if the dogs are unwilling to recognize all of them as important.

Jeeves reminded the dogs that if they don't take time to welcome these men and others like them, they probably won't stay.

And, then they will be transients.

🐾 PAINTED BLACK...

Jeeves enjoyed Thanksgiving.

He hopes everyone enjoyed the holiday too.

Jeeves learned that the day after Thanksgiving means more to some than the holiday does to him.

The day after is called "Black Friday."

"Black Friday" is a shopping day that can start as early as midnight.

Jeeves wonders why anyone would prefer a day called "black" that includes shopping over a holiday called "Thanksgiving" that usually includes lots of food.

Black is usually associated with death and mourning.

Black is often associated with a dark mood.

Black has also been associated with the plague.

Black also means the absence of light or color.

But Jeeves discovered that "Black Friday" signifies the time of year in which retail businesses expect to become profitable.

From Black Friday until the end of the year, retail business balance sheets are supposed to move from showing losses, which are usually depicted in red ink, to showing profits, which are usually depicted in black ink.

In this context, Jeeves understands why black can be a more attractive color than red.

Jeeves would have chosen green rather than black ink.

After all, green is the color of money.

Jeeves congratulates all businesses - small, medium and large.

He hopes that all are profitable, regardless of size.

But he worries about businesses that depend on the last Thursday of November to begin showing black ink.

Based on everything that Jeeves has read, it is more difficult for small businesses to be profitable.

From Dr. Chad Moutray, he learned that small business is viewed as the engine that drives our country's economy.

Dr. Moutray is chief economist for the Office of Advocacy, an independent voice for small business within our federal government's Small Business Administration (SBA.gov).

SBA defines a small business as one with 500 or less employees or $7 million or less in annual receipts.

According to Dr. Moutray, "Small businesses accounted for 65 percent of the 15 million net new jobs created between 1993 and 2009. Small business drives the American economy. Main Street provides the jobs and spurs our economic growth. American entrepreneurs are creative and productive, and these numbers prove it."

Jeeves believes that most Lincoln businesses are small businesses.

And many of them are retail businesses.

He also believes that small business drives this city's economy too.

Jeeves can't imagine having to work for 328 days just for the chance to make a profit.

And he can't imagine having to work so long with no guarantee that the last 37 days of this year will bring prosperity.

It's tough to be in business - anywhere - including Lincoln.

Yet, this year, city of Lincoln's finance department reports that it received 446 applications for business licenses from Jan. 1 to Nov. 28, 2011.

Jeeves looks forward to seeing more new business come to Lincoln in 2012.

He can hardly wait for Cool Hand Luke's to open its doors early next year.

Cool Hand Luke's will be housed in the former Beermann's Restaurant, which has been closed for almost six years.

Jeeves has already looked at the Cool Hand Luke's website, coolhandlukes.com.

While there, Jeeves peeked at the menus.

They made his tail wag.

Alas, neither Jeeves nor any other dog will be allowed in this or any other downtown restaurant.

But he's pretty certain that he will be allowed to sample any leftovers.

That's good enough for Jeeves.

He will be happy to wait any number of days for the chance to taste what's left.

But he hopes that no Lincoln businesses will have to wait more than 300 days until they see black ink.

Jeeves will try to help by continuing to spend his allowance in Lincoln.

At this time of year, he will also devote some of his money to buy items to drop in Toys for Tots boxes.

If he has any left over, he will buy See's Candy from Kiwanis Club of Lincoln.

In that way, he hopes that local businesses and at least two charitable organizations will benefit.

But Jeeves knows that his budget is not enough to keep this city's business engine moving.

It will take support by both residents and visitors not only at this time of year but throughout the year.

For now, Lincoln's business engine is a compact one.

Based on what he has seen, Jeeves knows that it's well-tuned and efficient.

With a steady stream of fuel, it can be kept running on all cylinders.

As more businesses discover Lincoln, Jeeves expects our city's business engine to become turbo-charged.

When that happens, Jeeves hopes to see it painted green.

Meanwhile, he'll be happy to see it painted black.

It can be a more attractive color than red.

🐾 SMALL MERCIES...

Jeeves is a little dog.

He weighs less than 8 pounds and stands less than one foot high.

Jeeves could hardly wait for Small Business Saturday.

He likes any event that takes small into account.

Jeeves was surprised to learn that Small Business Saturday was developed by American Express.

There's nothing small about American Express.

According to the *Nilson Report*, it's the second largest credit-card company in the United States.

American Express overtook Master Card last year.

Nonetheless, Jeeves is happy that a large corporation promotes small business.

And he's even happier that so many shoppers took time out of their busy Saturday to support Lincoln's small businesses.

Many were first-time visitors to downtown Lincoln.

Jeeves hopes that they'll return.

Others were frequent visitors to downtown Lincoln.

Some refer to these visitors as regulars.

Jeeves likes regulars.

And he especially likes small ones.

Nine month old Cadence Carlson is a favorite.

Cadence regularly visits downtown Lincoln with her Grandparents Sue and Bob Carlson.

She doesn't say much but Jeeves knows that she loves downtown by the size of her smile.

Cadence may be small but she is the happiest little girl in the world.

Three year old Iris Wyatt is a favorite too.

Iris regularly visits downtown Lincoln with her Grandparents Sylvia and Ron Wyatt.

During her last visit, she explained to Jeeves that her Dad, Josh Wyatt, is a "pa-le-on-tol-o-gist."

Jeeves can hardly say paleontologist much less spell it.

But he would like to be with Iris' Dad when he uncovers really big bones.

Four-and-one-half year old Madison Olsen is another favorite.

Madison regularly visits downtown Lincoln with her Mother Wendy Olsen and her Grandmother Donna Judah.

If you're lucky, like Jeeves, she may even share a page from her coloring book.

Madison frequents downtown to the extent that she just asks for "my usual" when she places her lunch order.

And when she says "my usual," Simple Pleasures knows what she wants.

If you want to know what's in Madison's usual, stop by Simple Pleasures.

Cadence, Iris and Madison may be small in size.

But as far as Jeeves is concerned, there's nothing small about them.

Some may call them regulars.

But as far as Jeeves is concerned, there's nothing regular about them.

Cadence, Iris and Madison are extraordinary.

They've already discovered the joys of downtown Lincoln.

🐾 DECISIONS, DECISIONS...

Jeeves has a challenge.

He faces it every year.

He calls it his Christmas card conundrum.

Jeeves likes to send holiday greetings to his friends.

But, it's difficult to know which cards to buy.

Stores offer so many types, colors and styles.

And, cards vary in price.

But, cost is not a determining factor for Jeeves.

He wants his card to reflect his sentiments for the season.

And, Jeeves wants his recipients to know how much they mean to him.

It's difficult to choose.

He's tempted to buy cards with a picture of a Yorkshire Terrier on the front.

But, he runs the risk of disappointing friends of different breeds and species.

He's tempted to buy religious cards.

But, he runs the risk of disappointing friends of different faiths or no beliefs at all.

He's tempted to buy cards that say "Merry Christmas."

But, he runs the runs the risk of disappointing friends who celebrate Hanukkah or Kwanzaa.

He's tempted to buy cards that say "Seasons Greetings."

But, he runs the risk of disappointing friends who celebrate Christmas.

It's difficult to choose.

Then there's the matter of card colors.

Jeeves finds that most cards are green, red and gold.

These are traditional.

But, Jeeves saw some cards in black and silver.

These are avant garde.

It's difficult to choose.

Then, there's the matter of card style.

Some cards have humorous messages.

Jeeves likes to receive these types of cards.

Yet, he's not sure that his friends have similar tastes.

Some cards have serious messages.

Some cards have obscure messages.

It's difficult to choose.
Some cards are plain.
Some cards are fancy.
It's difficult to choose.
Some cards are small.
Some cards are large.
And, some cards are medium size.
A card that's too small may be lost in the mail.
A card that's too large may require extra postage.
It's difficult to choose.
Jeeves found cards that don't come in small, medium and large.
And, these cards don't require postage either.
These are Internet cards.
But, he also found that the selection of Internet cards is just as large as in stores.
It's difficult to choose.
Jeeves knows that he will have to overcome his Christmas card conundrum.
He'll buy his cards this week.
He'll meet the challenge.
He'll choose cards that reflect his sentiments.
And no matter which card his friends receive, Jeeves hopes that his friends know how much they mean to him.

🐾 SEATBELTS FASTENED...

Jeeves enjoys spending time with the downtown dogs.

He also enjoys spending time with downtown residents.

Last week, he saw his friend Andy McMurtrie.

Andy was volunteering her time on behalf of the new art association, Art League of Lincoln.

She was busy looking for places in which Lincoln's actors could perform.

Jeeves enjoys watching live performances.

And he knows Lincoln has many fine actors.

He likes actors.

Jeeves is especially fond of Bette Davis.

He wishes she was still around for live performances.

On rainy days, Jeeves enjoys curling up on his afghan and watching any movie with Bette Davis.

His favorite is the 1950s *All About Eve* in which Davis plays Margot Channing.

Early in the film, she delivers the famous line "Fasten your seat belts. It's going to be a bumpy night."

This line is an early warning sign of what is to come during the rest of the film.

Jeeves is happy about Art League of Lincoln and that it's embracing all artists, including actors.

More than 250 members came together to form the art league.

Recently, Art League of Lincoln received approval from Internal Revenue Service to operate as a nonprofit organization.

Jeeves was disheartened when Lincoln Arts and Culture Foundation closed its doors last February.

Although he wasn't surprised.

Early warning signs prompted more than 200 individuals to sign a petition for an audit in 2010.

Sadly, those warning signs and the petition were ignored.

And Lincoln Arts had many bumpy nights and days until its demise earlier this year.

Jeeves was frustrated to learn that Art League of Lincoln was unable to realize any assets from Lincoln Arts, including its Feats of Clay.

But the laws for dissolution of a nonprofit organization and distribution of any assets are clear.

To be eligible for any assets, a group must be an active nonprofit organization.

Jeeves now understands why any assets, including Feats of Clay, went to Placer Arts rather than Art League of Lincoln.

PlacerArts was active.

Art League of Lincoln was not yet active.

Thankfully, Art League of Lincoln is now active.

And Jeeves likes that Art League of Lincoln has come up with new and exciting ways to promote the arts in Lincoln.

Unlike its predecessor, Art League of Lincoln doesn't have a place to call home - a place where it can showcase Lincoln's artists.

But it doesn't matter.

Art League of Lincoln is promoting "phantom galleries."

Lincoln Boulevard businesses serve as "phantom galleries" and now feature the works of local artists.

Jeeves also like that Art League of Lincoln is bringing back Lincoln's premier art attraction, which is also known throughout the world.

Art League of Lincoln is calling it America's ClayFest.

America's ClayFest will take place next April 26 through May 26.

An opening night reception is set for Saturday, April 20 at Gladding, McBean

Based on everything that it has accomplished to date, Jeeves is confident that Art League of Lincoln needs no seat belts, just enthusiastic support.

Unfortunately, neither the city's nights and nor its days may run as smoothly.

Jeeves hopes that Lincoln City Manager Jim Estep will continue to keep the city steady as he has in the past.

But it may be tough for him.

Jeeves was shocked when he read the front page of last week's *Lincoln News Messenger* regarding a violation of the Brown Act.

He knows that when there is a breach of trust by anyone - in friendships, in families, in business and in government - the breach causes all participants to suffer.

In this instance, the violation of one Councilman affected all Councilmen.

Jeeves hopes the culprit is identified and comes forth to apologize so that trust can be restored to City Council.

He views this breach as an early warning sign of things to come.

And last week's *Lincoln News Messenger* front page portended more.

It revealed that "Interim Police Chief Paul Shelgren leaves February and that "Teacher's rep scolds city."

Both literally and metaphorically, Jeeves is closer to the ground than others.

Metaphorically, he can feel the earth shifting under his feet and can sense a change in barometric pressure.

These are warning signs that neither the U.S. Geological Survey nor National Hurricane Center can predict.

Yet these signs make Jeeves more uncomfortable than any calamity that any government agency can monitor or Mother Nature can unleash.

So he's storing extra kibble, digging up bones and battening down his bed.

Jeeves senses that Lincoln is in for some bumpy nights and bumpy days in the weeks and months ahead.

He's already fastened his seat belt.

🐾 SIZE DOESN'T MATTER...

Jeeves has a problem.

He understands his problem may be widespread.

The problem is called spam.

It's not the Spam that comes in a can.

It's the spam that comes to your email address.

In addition to his website, Jeeves has his own email address.

Every day, he receives email messages.

Usually, he recognizes the name of the sender.

He reads these messages right away.

But, sometimes new names pop up.

Jeeves reads these message too.

He often finds that these messages make no sense to him at all.

Jeeves wonders know why anyone would want to sell him drugs to enhance his masculinity.

He doesn't need to get any closer to trees, bushes and fire hydrants.

Jeeves wonders know why anyone would want to wire him money.

He doesn't have a bank account.

Jeeves wonders why anyone from the Bahamas would include him in a last will and testament.

He has never been more than 120 miles from Lincoln.

Jeeves wonders why anyone would think he needs a dating service to meet "hot chicks in your area."

He already has play dates with neighborhood dogs Cindy and Molly.

And, who plays with chickens?

And, why are they hot?

Fortunately, Jeeves' email service provider offers a way for him to report spam.

Jeeves reports at least 20 to 30 spam messages per week.

He hopes that these reports will one day make a difference

Meanwhile, Jeeves was exposed to something different via the Internet.

Instead of spam, it's called a scam.

This scam involves unscrupulous people who seek out their prey on websites like Craigslist.

A few weeks ago, Jeeves decided to sell some things that he no longer needs.

He was looking to raise some cash to buy gifts for the special dogs in his life.

Jeeves advertised his items for sale on Craigslist.

He was happy to receive an email with an offer to pay full price for one item even though the prospective buyer had not seen it.

Additionally, this buyer was prepared to pay Jeeves an additional $30 while he waited for the certified check to arrive.

Jeeves was so excited.

It sounded too good to be true.

To be on the safe side, Jeeves checked the Internet.

He opened the Google website on his computer.

In the search area, he typed "Craigslist buyers that offer to pay $30 more than asked."

Jeeves was shocked by what he discovered.

The offer was too good to be true.

It was a scam.

Jeeves was disappointed that he didn't make a sale.

But, he's happy that he didn't become a victim of a scam.

For now, he'll just have to endure spam.

And, he'll have to make do without wire transfers and foreign inheritances.

But, he can enjoy his play dates.

Like the trees, the bushes and the fire hydrants, Jeeves' girlfriends don't care about the size of his wallet.

🐾 LINE TIME...

Jeeves likes December.

At this time of year, the dogs hold their annual holiday party.

During the party, they play a game called one-liners.

This game involves remembering who is associated with a famous "line."

The dog that comes up with the most correct answers wins.

There's no prize except recognition as a champion.

Jeeves was discharged with developing this year's one-liners list.

He found some lines made famous by comedians.

And, he found some lines from television.

But, he found the best lines from movies.

In the spirit of the holiday season, Jeeves kicked off the contest with an easy one.

Who said, "Ho! Ho! Ho!"

The dogs yelled in unison "Santa Claus!"

Jeeves moved on to comedians.

He asked who prefaces his act with "You might be a redneck...?"

The dogs answered "Jeff Foxworthy."

Then Jeeves asked who said "I don't get no respect?"

They remembered that Rodney Dangerfield is known for this catch-phrase.

When it came to television, the dogs did equally well.

The younger dogs struggled with "Lucy! I'm Home!"

But, the older dogs remembered that this line came from Desi Arnaz as Ricky Ricardo in *I Love Lucy*.

And, the older dogs also remembered who said "Would you believe..."

It was Don Adams as Maxwell Smart in *Get Smart*.

The same was true for "I kid you not."

The older dogs remembered that this line is associated with television host Jack Parr.

All the dogs remembered, "Here's Johnny."

And, they remembered that it was Ed McMahon who said this line when he introduced Johnny Carson at the start of *The Tonight Show*.

Jeeves then switched to movie lines.

"Go ahead make my day."

The dogs are Clint Eastwood fans.

So, all remembered that he first said this line as Inspector Harry Callahan in *Sudden Impact*.

The dogs also love Marlon Brando films.

So it was easy for them to remember that "I coulda' been a contender" came from Brando as he played Terry Malloy in *On the Waterfront*.

"Fasten your seatbelts. It's going to be a bumpy night."

That line was another easy one for the dogs.

They recalled that Bette Davis said this line as Margo Channing in *All About Eve*.

They also remembered who said "All right, Mr. De Mille. I'm ready for my closeup."

It was Gloria Swanson as Norma Desmond in *Sunset Boulevard*.

Jeeves asked them who said "A martini. Shaken, not stirred?"

They remembered it was Sean Connery as James Bond in *Goldfinger*.

Jeeves tried to challenge the dogs with a more obscure movie line -"Leave the gun. Take the cannoli."

But they remembered it was Richard Castellano as Peter Clemenza in the "Godfather."

He tried to stump the dogs with "Follow the money.... Just follow the money."

But they remembered it was said by Deep Throat in *All the Presidents' Men* although they couldn't remember who played the part.

And they knew that "You talkin' to me?" was delivered by Robert DeNiro as Travis Bickle in *Taxi Driver*.

"I'll alert the media" was no challenge for the dogs.

They remembered John Gieldgud said this line as Hobson in *Arthur*.

And the dogs laughed at Jeeves when he asked what character is associated with "My momma always said life was like a box of chocolates. You never know what you're gonna get."

They told Jeeves that everybody remembers who made that line famous.

It was Tom Hanks as Forrest Gump in the movie of the same name.

Jeeves wrapped up the movie section with a line from a classic holiday movie "Look, Daddy. Teacher says, 'Every time a bell rings, an angel gets his wings.'"

The dogs remembered that the line came from *It's a Wonderful Life*.

They remembered that it was said by Zuzu Bailey to George Bailey.

Some even remembered that Karolyn Grimes played the part of Zuzu in the movie.

No matter how hard he tried, Jeeves couldn't stump the dogs.

But he saved the best for last and ended the contest with "Merry Christmas."

The dogs were perplexed.

In their estimation "Merry Christmas" didn't qualify as a one liner.

They reminded Jeeves that almost everyone says "Merry Christmas" at this time of year.

The dogs didn't understand why Jeeves would put "Merry Christmas" on the list.

A couple of dogs said that they associate "Merry Christmas" with family and friends.

A few other dogs said that "Merry Christmas" means gifts.

The dogs seemed disappointed in Jeeves for his addition to the contest list.

Jeeves was disappointed too.

He couldn't understand how the dogs could associate comedy, television and movie lines, yet they couldn't associate "Merry Christmas."

Jeeves believes that "Merry Christmas" is the best line of all time.

And, Jeeves has no difficulty remembering to whom and to what event he associates it.

In the true spirit of this season, he hopes that others remember too.

Merry Christmas!

🐾 'TWAS...

(Based on "A Visit from St. Nicholas" by Clement Clarke Moore)
'Twas a few days before Christmas, when all through the city
Not a Councilman was stirring, oh what a pity.
They had hung out the Art League and an attorney with nary a care,
While they hoped that a new City Manager soon would be there.
The Councilmen had nestled all smug in their heads,
While the rest of Lincoln looked to be led.
Jeeves and the dogs dressed in warm sweaters,
Were sitting in Beermann Plaza hoping for better.
When out on Fifth Street, they heard such a clatter,
They jumped up on all fours to see what was the matter.
When what to their wondering eyes did appear,
Another food truck event to make them sneer.
No miniature sleigh, no tiny reindeer,
Just business interlopers with nothing to fear.
But then in a twinkling, the dogs heard a sound;
Down Lincoln Boulevard, St. Nicholas came with a bound.
He stopped at Buonarroti's to wish Daniel well;
Then, he went on to Simple Pleasures with a story to tell.
"Don't worry," he said, "those food trucks won't last,"
"As soon as Beermann's has a new tenant, they'll be a thing of the past."
With a wink of his eye and a twist of his head,
He let us know we had nothing to dread.
His eyes-how they twinkled! His dimples, how merry!
"And, some day," he said, "you'll have a full-time library."
He spoke not another word but went straight to his work;
And, he wrote a new sign ordinance with not so much as a quirk.
Then he sprang to his sleigh and as he drove out of sight,
Jeeves heard him exclaim "Merry Christmas and to all a Good Night!"

🐾 IN A LAND CALLED HONNAH LEE…

Jeeves took time out over the holidays.

He watched televison.

Saturday morning, Jeeves watched a two-hour show over Public Broadcasting System.

The show was called *50 Years of Peter, Paul and Mary*.

It was a great show.

Jeeves heard this trio sing songs that he rarely hears.

He heard them sing John Denver's "Leaving on a Jet Plane."

He heard them sing Bob Dylan's "Blowin' In the Wind."

He heard them sing Gordon Lightfoots' "Early Morning Rain."

He heard them sing Phil Och's "There But for Fortune."

He heard them sing Pete Seeger's "Where Have All the Flowers Gone?"

And, he heard them sing his favorite, by Leonard Lipton and Peter Yarrow, "Puff the Magic Dragon."

These are known as songs that inspired a generation.

And, fifty years ago, Peter, Paul and Mary helped lead a generation in non violent civil rights marches in Washington, D.C. and Selma, Alabama.

They also tweaked our national consciousness regarding the war in Viet Nam and injustices in El Salvador.

But no matter what anyone may think about their political views, Jeeves believes that Peter, Paul and Mary make up an important part of America's songbook.

Their harmonies and their songs are unmistakable.

So, he not surprised that PBS would pay tribute to Peter, Paul and Mary.

PBS also celebrated 25 years of Peter, Paul and Mary in 1986 with a special broadcast.

Sadly, Mary Travers died in 2009 after a 5-year battle with leukemia.

Happily, we have her recorded voice along with Peter Yarrow and Paul Stookey to enjoy in perpetuity.

Both Peter Yarrow and Paul Stookey continue to perform and support worthwhile causes.

Peter Yarrow established a non profit called *Operation Respect*.

According to its website OperationRespect.org, Yarrow's organization works to assure that children have "a respectful, safe and compassionate climate of learning where their academic, social and emotional development can take place free of bullying, ridicule and violence."

To date, over 40,000 educators have participated in *Operation Respect* workshops throughout the United States.

And, Paul Stookey co-founded *Hugworks* that uses original musical compositions as music therapy to address the special needs of children.

Hugworks has produced three award-winning children's CDs used in hospitals, medical camps and homes across the country.

Jeeves wonders which artists PBS will select and pay tribute fifty years from now.

And, he wonders which artists will tweak the American consciousness through their songs.

Peter, Paul and Mary are known for "If I had a Hammer" (Pete Seeger).

Current pop star Miley Cyrus is known for "Wrecking Ball" (Sacha Skarbek).

Miley Cyrus is also known for twerking but not for tweaking.

By any standards, Jeeves believes that "twerking" is a sad legacy.

Jeeves hears no voices that inspire him like Peter, Paul and Mary.

Instead, he hears protesters call for violent actions against police that are unworthy of any attention.

He wonders if rappers like Jay Z, or pop stars Lady Gaga and Miley Cyrus will stand the same test of time as Peter, Paul and Mary.

Will these new artists make up what we call the American songbook?

Jeeves believes the answer may be "Blowin' In the Wind."

🐾 BY A NOSE...

Jeeves looks forward to 2015.

He's buried a few bones.

He's dug up some old ones.

And, he's kept a couple that still have a little meat left to chew.

Jeeves also plans to sniff out some new and meatier bones.

He likes to sniff.

In Beermann Plaza, both he and the Downtown Dogs find new scents during every visit.

Some smells are pleasant and some smells are foul.

After a food truck event, their noses are overloaded by the smells of all that has been left behind.

Those smells are foul.

Jeeves and the dogs take comfort from the pleasant odors that emanate from Los Gallos Taqueria and Simple Pleasures restaurants.

They also miss the odor from Beermann's Restaurant when it smoked meat.

And, they miss the odor from Knee Deep Brewery when it made beer.

They were pleasant smells too.

Jeeves and the Downtown Dogs hope these two businesses will soon be replaced by new ones.

They keep sniffing but have yet to get a whiff of new tenants despite the rumors.

Jeeves learned that dogs' noses can detect smells better than human noses.

The smallest dog has a more sensitive nose than the largest human.

Jeeves first made this discovery when he read *Inside of a Dog* by Alexander Horowitz (Scribner, 2009).

Unlike human beings, he learned that dogs do not become accustomed to smells, good or bad.

A dog has 125 to 300 million scent glands.

A human has about five million scent glands.

So, a dog's sense of smell is much more sensitive than a human's sense of smell.

Jeeves learned even more when he read a December 8, 2014 column in *Telegraph Magazine* (www.telegraph.co.uk) called "Pet Rescue" by Louise Carpenter.

In her column, Ms. Carpenter writes about medical detection dogs that are being trained to sniff out illnesses such as diabetes, cancer and allergies.

In 2004, *BMJ* (British Medical Journal) published a medical paper about dogs that were detecting bladder cancer.

Since then, more work has been done in the United Kingdom and throughout the world.

U.K. psychologist Dr. Claire Guest set up a charity called Medical Detection Dogs in 2008 (http://medicaldetectiondogs.org.uk).

Her Royal Highness the Duchess of Cornwall is a patron.

Medical Detection Dogs has two parts - Medical Alert Assistance Dogs and Cancer Detection Dogs.

The assistance part trains dogs to help owners manage their diseases.

The detection part trains dogs to sniff out certain cancers through changes in urine or breath.

More than 50 dogs have been trained to smell the changes in breath due to type 1 diabetes.

And, fifteen dogs are in training to "sniff out changes in urine produced by prostate, bladder and urinary cancers."

The types of dogs vary.

They can be Labrador Retrievers, Cocker Spaniels and French Poodles.

Jeeves was delighted to read that a Yorkshire Terrier puppy called "Buddy" has been recruited.

Medical Detection Dogs was selected as *The Telegraph's* choice for its 2014 Christmas charitable appeal.

A "Google" search revealed that other countries such as Germany and Israel are conducting research into the accuracy of dog sniffing concerning certain cancers including ovarian cancer.

In the United States, Dogs4Diabetics was founded in 2004 (www.dogs4diabetics.com) which teaches dogs how to sniff out hypoglycemia in insulin dependent diabetic patients.

In Canada's capital city of Ottawa, a non profit organization called "CancerDogs" (www.cancerdogs.ca) is training dogs to detect the biochemical traces of cancer the same way other dogs are trained to detect traces of explosives or drugs.

Another Canadian organization called "Trailrunners" has been working with Labrador Retrievers in Saskatchewan to teach them how to detect cancer smells (www.cancerdogs.com).

Jeeves knows that all research efforts with respect to dog sniffs are in the early stages of development.

Neither he nor the Downtown Dogs plan to set up a medical clinic in Beermann Plaza.

Jeeves also knows that sniffing is not going to replace the stethoscope, laboratory tests, x-rays and all other forms of current medical examination and detection.

But, he does believe that dogs may offer another tool in the arsenal against illness.

And, Jeeves makes no bones about it, this new tool is something to sniff at.

🐾 PROBLEMATIC...

Jeeves has a problem.

And, when he has a problem, he usually consults the Downtown Dogs.

This time, he decided to contact the neighborhood dogs first.

Jeeves met with his friend Molly.

She, like Jeeves, lives in Sun City.

"What's the problem?" asked Molly.

Jeeves told Molly that he has been invited to be a "Celebrity Waiter" by Lighthouse Counseling & Family Resource Center for its May 19, 2017 annual fund raising luncheon.

Molly asked "What's a celebrity? And, what's a waiter?"

"That's the problem!" said Jeeves "I don't know anything about either."

Molly was equally perplexed.

She said "My best guess is that a celebrity is someone who is celebrated."

"And, if that's the case, it eliminates both you and me."

"After all, neither you nor I are well-known like Lassie, Benji, Rin Tin Tin, Toto or Old Yeller."

As to being a waiter, Molly also didn't understand why anyone or any dog would want to sit around and wait much less why such activity would be cause for celebration.

"As you know Jeeves, I am not in the habit of waiting for anyone or anything."

Jeeves left his meeting with Molly more confused than ever.

He decided to call his friend Nasha.

Like Jeeves, Nasha is a terrier but she's a Scottish Terrier rather than a Yorkshire Terrier.

And, like Molly and Jeeves, Nasha lives in Sun City.

Nasha mulled over Jeeves problem.

After a few minutes in her best brogue, she said "nay, A'm sairy wee laddie, I canna give ye an answer."

Jeeves now realized that, if he wanted answers, it was time to call for a meeting of the Downtown Dogs.

The dogs gathered around the fountain in Beermann Plaza.

Jeeves explained his problem to them.

"First of all," said Luna "you should be honored to be invited to this luncheon."

"Did they give you any more information?"

Jeeves circulated the flyer that is available on Lighthouse's website, http://lighthousefrc.org.

After carefully reviewing the form, Spike said, "Last year, most of the Celebrity Waiters were elected officials."

The Downtown Dogs laughed.

"Why are you laughing?" asked Jeeves.

"That luncheon may be as close as any of those officials ever get to actually serving the public," chuckled Mabel.

"After they are elected, some politicians often spend more time dining out on their victories rather than working on behalf of their constituents."

"But," remarked Lexi, "they're good at raising money!"

Jeeves reminded the dogs that the luncheon was not designed to promote elected officials or help them raise money.

Instead, it was designed to raise awareness and much needed funds for the many important services that Lighthouse provides.

As such, Jeeves implored the dogs to give this event their serious attention.

"You're right, Jeeves" said Luna. "It's time for us to more fully assess the situation."

The dogs wondered aloud why Jeeves was asked over other local celebrities.

Lexi said "While you may write a bi-weekly column for *Lincoln News Messenger*, your Editor Carol Feineman and Reporter Steve Archer have greater stature and celebrity status than you."

Jeeves agreed.

He wondered why Lighthouse didn't ask them or one of the weekly and better known columnists like Jane Tahti?

"And, what do you know about being a waiter, Jeeves?" asked Luna.

"Nothing," said Jeeves. "That's why I called this meeting."

The dogs explained that waiting on tables meant taking plates of food from the kitchen and setting them down before each attendee.

And, they went on to explain that because attendees will buy tickets for the luncheon, they will expect good service.

"That means you can't sneak food off plates, drool on them or spill anything!" remarked Spike.

As a food lover, Jeeves didn't know if he could manage.

Luna asked "how good are you at standing and walking on your hind legs while you carry a plate of food?"

"I've never done it" said Jeeves.

"Perhaps I could take lessons from the servers at Beermann's, Simple Pleasures or Buonarroti's?"

The Downtown Dogs agreed that might be a good idea.

But then, Spike reminded Jeeves that, as a dog, even a celebrity dog, he is prohibited from going into restaurants.

"Unless this event is being held on a patio, you can't attend."

"I forgot all about that issue," lamented Jeeves.

"As far as I know, the luncheon is being held indoors at Orchard Creek Lodge in Sun City Lincoln Hills."

Sadly, both he and the Downtown Dogs agreed that Jeeves would be unable to participate in the Celebrity Waiter Luncheon.

"It's a sad day for all of us," said Luna.

"I thought that at least one of could have done duty as a service dog."

"But, let's not despair," she said. " Jeeves, you can continue to promote Lighthouse's luncheon in your column."

"Good idea!" exclaimed the other dogs in unison.

"And, we can continue to spread the word to all the other dogs including your neighborhood friends!"

"If we bark loud and often enough, we'll get our owners to pay attention."

"And, if we nip at their heels, they're sure to buy tickets to the luncheon."

Although disappointed by what the Downtown Dogs had told him, Jeeves's problem was finally solved.

Alas, he knew that he wasn't a celebrity and that he couldn't be a waiter.

But he knew that he could help find sponsors, solicit donations and sell tickets to Lighthouse Counseling & Family Resource Center's Annual Celebrity Waiter Luncheon on May 17.

For Jeeves, that's a problem even he can solve.

🐾 HOLES IN ONE...

Sometimes, Jeeves finds that there more events than there is space in this column.

Other times, Jeeves doesn't hear about events until after they have occurred.

Regardless, he is always grateful to discover that Lincoln residents are busy - within this city's borders and beyond.

Jeeves wishes that he could attend everything and go everywhere.

He would like to be known as a party animal.

That's not possible.

He's just a little dog on a short leash.

Just the same, he lives an exciting life.

Most of it, he lives vicariously through many of Lincoln's brightest and best.

Jeeves wishes he could spend more time with Nina Mazzo.

He would like to help her pick out the doughnuts that she takes to the volunteers at Friends of Lincoln Library's book sales.

He likes Nina, Friends of Lincoln Library and books even more than he likes doughnuts.

They're better for him too.

He wonders why there are doughnut holes.

Who made them and why?

Perhaps Nina could help him find out.

Jeeves wishes be could accompany Nina to the next World Mystery Convention, commonly referred to as *Boucheron*, named to honor mystery fiction critic, editor and author, Anthony Boucher.

Nina attended the most recent convention in St. Louis, MO.

Next year's will be held in Cleveland, OH where best selling mystery writer Mary Higgins Clark will be honored.

Maybe Mary Higgins Clark could help him solve the mystery of holes in doughnuts.

But no dogs are allowed.

Closer to home, Jeeves wishes he could have attended the recent party at the home of Therese and Mark Adams.

The party was for women only.

No dogs were allowed, regardless of gender.

Over 70 guests were on-hand to celebrate the accomplishments and contributions of women and what would have been the 105th birthday of Therese's late grandmother.

No doughnuts were served.

But caterer Laura Kenny was on-hand to showcase her culinary skills.

Jeeves has been able to savor Laura's specialties through recipes from the cookbook, *Placer County Real Food,* that she co-authored with Joanne Neft.

Everyone enjoyed a spectacular meal, under the stars, while sipping wines from Rancho Roble Vineyards - lots and lots of wine.

Everyone included friends who are real Placer grown - Dr. Lyndell Grey of Old Fruitvale School and Jane Tahti.

Jeeves learned that Jane Tahti once held the title of Miss Placer County - one item on a long list of accomplishments.

Jeeves wishes that he could have witnessed first-hand Therese Adams doing renditions of hits from her favorite musical, *Mama Mia.*

Alas, he's no dancing queen either.

That's why he wishes that he could go line-dancing with his friend, Susan Joyce.

In addition to being an accomplished vocalist who generously volunteers her talents at many Lincoln events, Susan line dances.

But his friend, Downtown Dog Buster, reminded Jeeves that he has two left feet.

Besides, no dogs are allowed.

Jeeves wishes he could join Jeri Chase Ferris on stage when she performs along with cast mates from Lincoln Hills Players' Group in *Christmas Belles.*

Then, he could take direction from Elly Award-winning director Diane Bartlett.

But no dogs are allowed.

Jeeves wishes that he could have accompanied the members of The Lincoln Hills Photography Group to San Francisco when they took their photos of Golden Gate Bridge.

He also wishes he could have attended the opening exhibit of those photographs and reception at Mina's Coffee House.

But no dogs were allowed.

One day, he hopes the group takes photographs of doughnuts.

That would be a great exhibit too.

Jeeves wishes that he could have accompanied Councilman Tom Cosgrove to Calgary, Alberta.

Jeeves has never been to Canada.

As a member of Sacramento Area Council of Governments, Councilman Cosgrove was invited to participate on a panel.

It's an honor that recognizes his committee service and accomplishments.

Jeeves wonders if Councilman Cosgrove tried any Canadian doughnuts and if they have holes.

He also wonders if Councilman Cosgrove saw any chuck wagon races that are an integral part of the annual Calgary Stampede.

Maybe Lincoln could have a stampede.

Maybe Lincoln could have chuck wagon races.

And maybe dogs would be allowed.

When Councilman Cosgrove returns, Jeeves will ask..

Meanwhile, Jeeves has much to discover right here in Lincoln not the least of which is who made doughnut holes and why.

That's a lot for a little dog on a short leash.

Pass the bagels please.

🐾 HOME AGAIN...

By now, most readers know that Jeeves was born in Lincoln.

It's his home town.

Lincoln is the only city that has ever known.

Sometimes, Jeeves hears Kathy reminisce about her old home town of Brampton.

It's located about 20 miles northwest of Toronto.

He wonders how Kathy could leave.

Jeeves could not imagine leaving Lincoln for another city.

He also wonders why she has no desire to return.

Perhaps it's as simple as Thomas Wolfe wrote, *You Can't Go Home Again*.

Yet Jeeves continues to wonder what she might be missing.

Some time ago, *Lincoln News Messenger* reporter Stephanie Dumm taught Jeeves how to use the Internet.

She also taught him how to access other community newspapers from around the world and how to retrieve local stories.

Based on her instructions, Jeeves conducted a Google search to learn about Kathy's former city

Once he found the local newspaper's website, Jeeves decided to poke around.

He wondered how Lincoln compares.

More importantly, Jeeves hoped to discover why Kathy prefers Lincoln over the city in which she grew up.

What he found out amused him.

In her former home town, Jeeves found that the issues there are pretty much the same except on a much larger scale.

It's to be expected.

Brampton city is more than 10 times larger than Lincoln.

Ironically, it's newspaper is smaller.

Jeeves wondered if it's because there's not much going on or if it's because the people have nothing to say.

Maybe that's why Kathy left.

Jeeves knows that Lincoln always has a lot going on and people here always have something to say.

Maybe that's why Kathy stays.

Jeeves dug deeper.

He discovered that just before Kathy left, in 1993, Brampton opened a new City Hall.

Jeeves discovered that it now has a big plans for downtown redevelopment that includes another new City Hall - all of which sounded familiar.

The cost of construction for this new building is estimated to be over $500 per square foot.

Yet that city's newspaper reports that cost of construction should be about $325 per square foot based on cost comparisons in the greater Toronto area.

Taxpayers are expressing concern over this cost differential.

Taxpayers are also expressing concern over the impact that a new City Hall will have on its historic area.

And there's bickering about that city's proposed 2012 budget.

Although it's supposed to be identical to 2011, the new budget will add an average of about $60 per year to the average property tax bill.

Needless to say, those residents are unhappy about paying more taxes.

This also sounded familiar.

But Jeeves found also learned about Brampton's plans for downtown redevelopment.

This part of the plan isn't going to cost a lot of money.

Jeeves likes those kinds of plans.

Brampton's city's councillors believe that "the future of the downtown core can be built on heritage, arts, culture and entertainment."

Already, they have a five-year goal to make it happen.

And they approved a five-year economic development plan in it's budget that will see city staff "pursue and promote the development of a creative economy in the city"

Jeeves was fascinated by the concept of a "creative economy."

He wondered what such an economy entails.

Once again, he searched Google.

Jeeves found that a creative economy is a big subject that has many aspects.

Simply stated, it's an economy based on ideas rather than industry.

Creative economies are replacing industrial economies.

Both Hollywood and Silicon Valley are two examples of a creative economy.

They're based on creative companies.

Mountain View based Google is one of them.

Jeeves also found that many cities throughout the world are pursuing this type of economy.

Lincoln may have an edge.

Our historic downtown already has Lincoln Arts and Culture Foundation at 580 6th Street..

And, by moving Lincoln Area Archives Museum to the former city hall at 640 5th Street where it is more visible and accessible, Lincoln may be on its way to developing its own kind of creative economy.

Jeeves learned a lot by searching the Internet.

He also discovered a map-search feature that can take you to the front door of just about any home.

As a result, Jeeves was able to find a satellite photo of Kathy's former residence.

He showed it to her.

Kathy was surprised to discover that it has a new stone facade, windows and landscaping.

Although she liked what she saw, it no longer reflects her tastes.

It's the home of others and reflects their tastes.

She reminded Jeeves that her home is now in Lincoln.

And she has no desire to return to Brampton.

Jeeves is happy to know that this is where she plans to stay.

Even so, Jeeves found out that you can go home again.

Thanks to Google, you don't even have to leave Lincoln.

🐾 BEWARE OF PINK...

Jeeves keeps reading and hearing a lot about "pink slips."

It's a subject he knows nothing about.

Last week, he decided to take it up with the Downtown Dogs.

However, they has already left Beermann Plaza to start their New Year's celebrations.

So Jeeves decided to scratch and sniff to find other sources.

A few city workers were walking through the plaza.

Jeeves asked them if they knew anything about "pink slips."

Their eyes grew very wide and they ran away with out answering him.

What about pink slips could conjure up such horror, Jeeves wondered.

Undeterred, Jeeves contacted Cindy, the little French poodle.

"Cindy, what is a pink slip?" Jeeves asked.

"Oo, la, la!" she exclaimed.

"Monsieur Jeeves, c'est lingerie."

"C'est something you wear under a dress - often seen in Paris but seldom seen in Lincoln."

Cindy suggested that Jeeves go to Victoria's Secret for more information.

Somehow, Jeeves knew that hers was not the appropriate direction for him to take.

How could a pretty item of under clothing elicit such fearful reactions?

Jeeves turned to his buddies, Buster and Diesel, and asked the same question.

But they just wanted the address of the French Poodle.

His daschund friend, Sweet Pea, didn't know the answer either.

He suggested that Jeeves visit the library.

Alas, he found the Carnegie Library closed.

How could this be?

Where was Jeeves going to find an answer to this most perplexing problem?

And, why was this essential city service unavailable during regular business hours?

The next day, Jeeves sat down at his computer and conducted an Internet search.

What he found made him growl and bark.

A pink slip is not an undergarment at all.

Instead, it's a euphemism for a lay-off from work.

Although the Smithsonian has never found an actual "pink slip," the expression has become synonymous with worker lay-offs.

How could such a pretty color come to be associated with something so frightful?

No wonder city employees ran away when he tried to ask them about "pink slips."

Lay-offs mean loss of income.

Without paychecks, how could city employees pay their mortgages, keep their medical benefits and feed their families?

Interestingly, when Jeeves looked up "pink slips," he also found references to "golden parachutes."

What he found out made his ears stand up, his nostrils flare and the air on his back bristle.

Golden parachutes are not something retirees wear when they sky dive.

Instead, a golden parachute is a euphemism for executive severance and benefits.

Golden parachutes have become synonymous with payouts that executives and upper echelons in management receive in order to depart, regardless of what they leave behind.

Jeeves was now more confounded than ever.

How did it come to pass that the employees who work at the direction of management wind up with nothing?

And, how did it come to pass that the ones who direct and are asked to depart wind up with more?

For Jeeves, getting a golden parachute would be like getting a treat for raising his leg against the dining room table.

He can hardly wait to discuss this with the Downtown Dogs.

None of it makes sense to Jeeves and none of it seems fair.

🐾 BED TIME...

Jeeves made a new acquaintance over the holidays.

Her name is Mollie.

She's a dachshund.

And she's older woman.

Jeeves met Mollie through his friend Cindy.

She's a french poodle.

And she's a younger woman.

The three dogs spent many days together.

Cindy and Jeeves like to play.

Mollie has no interest in playing with either of them.

But she does like to curl up in Jeeves' blanket and sleep in his bed.

Jeeves tries to be a gentleman.

He stands and wags his tail whenever a woman enters the room.

He takes off his leash and the hat that Margi Grant made him whenever he eats.

He shares his toys.

But Jeeves does not know what to do when another dog uses his blanket and occupies his bed.

So he consulted the Downtown Dogs.

They always know what to do.

And now that Luna the Country Dog has moved downtown, the dogs have gained a broader perspective.

The Downtown Dogs compared Jeeves current predicament to one that Lincoln faced about 12 years ago.

That's when a whole lot of old people, like Mollie, moved here.

According to the dogs, not only did they try to occupy our bed but some tried to remake it.

Their movement was different from the current occupy movement.

Unlike the current one, these old people both like and depend on Wall Street.

They're also used to fancy high count sheets, eiderdown duvets and adjustable comfort settings through sleep numbers on their king-sized mattresses.

A little while later, a lot of yuppies moved here too.

They also tried to occupy our bed and remake it.

They even tried to move Lincoln's railway line.

They're also used to fancy sheets and matching decorator comforter ensembles.

But they like the kind of king-sized mattresses on which they can set their wine in long-stemmed glasses without the risk of spills.

Unlike them, Lincoln has always been more used to cotton sheets, wool blankets, bedspreads and box-spring mattress sets.

Yet Lincoln's residents have always been every bit as warm and cozy as any newcomers.

The dogs told Jeeves about Goldilocks.

Just as Jeeves has endured Mollie and Lincoln has endured newcomers, the three bears endured her.

Not only did Goldilocks occupy their beds, she also ate their porridge.

The dogs hope that eventually everyone will find Lincoln's bed just right.

Meanwhile, they recommend that Jeeves continue to be polite.

He should respect his elders even if it means everyone over the age of 4.

If Mollie tries to occupy his bed again, Jeeves could take his protest to the street.

However, the dogs believe that it would be better and a lot warmer to crawl in beside her.

Jeeves may find that she makes it just right.

But he's not sure that he'll let Mollie eat his porridge no matter how old she is.

🐾 WALK WAYS...

Jeeves is a little dog on a short leash.

Some people call a leash a lead.

When Jeeves goes out for a walk, he doesn't lead.

Instead, he drags whoever is at the other end of the leash.

Developing good leadership skills is something Jeeves is working on.

So far, he's learned that good leadership is not something he can demand.

Jeeves now knows that it's earned.

Good leadership requires a variety of special attributes and skills.

Integrity and credibility are two attributes usually found at the top of any leadership list.

Communication skills are equally important.

Good leaders inspire and motivate.

Yet they can listen equally well.

Jeeves understand that if he barks and bites, people won't want to spend time with him.

If he can't be trusted to behave, people won't want to read his column in the *Lincoln News Messenger*.

Good leaders know how to prioritize.

They are decisive and have enviable track records.

Good leaders also accept responsibility for their decisions.

They can step back to reassess, re-evaluate and re-approach.

And they will admit their mistakes when they are wrong.

But Jeeves was surprised to discover that even if someone possesses all these positive traits, leadership is not guaranteed,

Many history books, from this country and around the world, recount the exploits of bad leaders.

They are usually the ones who used force and intimidation to get their way.

Those approaches don't work for long.

People will eventually rise up and remove bad leaders.

They will replace them with leaders who represent their ideals.

Getting people to follow is difficult.

Jeeves was reminded that if you set out on a path and there's no one behind, you are merely going on a solitary walk.

Jeeves believes that it is time for those who call themselves city leaders to look behind and see if anyone is following.

If they find no one, perhaps it's time for them to keep walking.

🐾 MAKE MINE A DOUBLE...

Jeeves loves Beermann Plaza.

On a sunny day, he can find no more pleasant spot.

He especially likes to sit on the edge of the fountain and feel the spray.

On a hot July day, there's nothing more refreshing.

While sitting there, Jeeves lets his mind wander.

He never knows where his thoughts will take him.

A few weeks go, he found himself thinking about *Sunshine Sketches of a Little Town* by Stephen Leacock.

Published in 1912, *Sunshine Sketches of a Little Town* is one of Jeeves' favorite books.

Anyone who enjoys Garrison Keillor's *Lake Wobegon Days* will enjoy Stephen Leacock's stories too.

Sunshine Sketches of a Little Town takes place in a fictional town called Mariposa.

Stephen Leacock tells us in the book's Preface that "Mariposa is not a real town. On the contrary, it is about seventy or eighty of them."

Jeeves likes to believe that Lincoln is one of them.

The first time he read the book, Jeeves discovered a new beverage called sarsaparilla.

He had never heard of this drink before.

Jeeves was fascinated by something called sarsaparilla although he found it difficult to pronounce.

And, Jeeves wondered about sarsaparilla's flavor.

Would it be sweet, bitter or sour?

So, he decided it was time to find a bottle and experience the taste.

First, Jeeves asked Downtown Dog Luna if she had ever tasted sarsaparilla.

"No," said Luna.

Then, Jeeves asked Luna is she knew where he could buy sarsaparilla.

"No," said Luna "but maybe Foto's Market has some."

Jeeves walked down Fifth Street to Foto's Market.

He checked all the shelves and the coolers but could find no sarsaparilla.

Jeeves was discouraged.

As he left Foto's he ran into Mabel the basset hound.

"Why don't you try Buonarroti's Ristorante?" she said.

So, Jeeves trotted back down Fifth Street, crossed over Lincoln Boulevard and entered Buonarroti's.

He stepped up to the bar and asked owner Daniel Alcantero if he could have a glass of sarsaparilla.

"I'm sorry Jeeves, I have no sarsaparilla," said Daniel "but I would be happy to make you a martini."

Jeeves was grateful for the offer.

He could imagine himself being like James Bond and saying "I'd like mine shaken not stirred."

But, Jeeves reminded himself that he was in search of sarsaparilla not a martini.

On his way back to Beermann Plaza, Jeeves ran into Luna again.

"How did you make out Jeeves?" Luna asked.

Jeeves explained that he couldn't find any sarsaparilla.

"It's difficult to find a lot of things in Lincoln since so many stores and restaurants have closed," she said.

But, Luna went on to suggest "Why don't you try Simple Pleasures?"

Jeeves went into Simple Pleasures and found Erica Burke behind the counter.

He asked her for some sarsaparilla.

Erica said, "you'll probably find a little sarsaparilla in our root beer."

Jeeves was so happy.

Not only did Erica knew about sarsaparilla, but she offered hope that he could actually taste it.

Alas, Jeeves read the label and found no sarsaparilla listed on the root beer bottle.

Disappointed, he went out the back door where Jeeves found Downtown Dog Buster sitting on Simple Pleasures patio.

"Why are you so forlorn?" asked Buster.

"I can't find sarsaparilla anywhere," said Jeeves.

Buster had never heard of sarsaparilla.

"Where did you learn about sarsaparilla? asked Buster.

Jeeves informed him that he read about sarsaparilla in a book called *Sunshine Sketches of a Little Town*.

"I'm unfamiliar with that book" said Buster. "When was it written?"

"I don't know when it was written but it was first published in 1912," said Jeeves.

Buster chuckled and reminded Jeeves that over 100 years have passed since this book was published and a lot has happened.

"Since then, we now have all kinds of drinks and countless varieties of bottled water," said Buster. "Why June 24, Lincoln City Council passed its Capital Improvement Budget that sets aside funds for a program to reclaim our water."

"I didn't know that our water was missing," said Jeeves.

Buster explained to Jeeves that our water hasn't been missing as much as the city had been missing out on an opportunity to recycle our wastewater.

Mayor Hydrick and city Councilmen Stan Nader and Spencer Short voted to support the Capital Improvement Budget.

As a result, City of Lincoln is going to treat our wastewater by removing solids and impurities so that it can be recycled for use in other ways such as irrigation.

Jeeves was excited about the prospect of recycling our water.

He and all the dogs have been careful to conserve water during this drought.

Jeeves wondered why the other two city Councilmen, Peter Gilbert and Paul Joiner, didn't support this opportunity to reclaim our water.

Jeeves can hardly wait for reclaimed water to start flowing.

He wonders if reclaimed water will be used to water the grass in Beermann Plaza.

He wonders if reclaimed water will be used in the fountain.

And, he wonders if the water will ever be treated enough so that he can drink it.

He'll never know if it tastes like sarsaparilla.

But, Jeeves does know that if he's ever offered a glass of reclaimed water, he'll have his shaken and stirred.

🐾 SWING AMONG THE STARS...

During the winter, Jeeves watches *American Idol*.

He enjoys hearing all the young people sing as they compete for a chance to gain a recording contract and become an American Idol.

Jeeves can bark.

Jeeves can growl.

But he can't sing.

During the summer, Jeeves watches *So You Think You can Dance*.

He enjoys watching young people dance as they compete to become known as America's best dancer.

Jeeves can walk.

Jeeves can run.

But he can't dance.

Jeeves has two left feet, literally.

What these two television shows have in common is great music.

As a result of watching both programs, Jeeves has become familiar with the music of Frank Sinatra.

Jeeves enjoys hearing his songs.

In particular, he likes "I've Got the World on a String."

This song conjures up all kinds of wonderful images for Jeeves.

He would love to have the world on a leash rather than be on the end of one.

After "I've Got the World on a String," Sinatra goes on to sing the second line, "I'm sittin' on a rainbow."

Jeeves has seen a rainbow in the sky.

Like Frank Sinatra, he would love to sit on one if only for a few seconds.

Jeeves wonders if it would be as nice as sitting around the fountain in Beermann Plaza.

Jeeves also likes to hear Frank Sinatra sing "Fly Me to the Moon."

He would love to go to the moon or even the space station.

But that's not possible.

Jeeves was disappointed to learn that the shuttle made its final journey into outer space.

After "Fly Me to the Moon," Sinatra goes on to sing the second line, "Let me swing among the stars."

Jeeves has seen stars in the sky.

Like Sinatra, he would love to swing among them if only for a few seconds.

Jeeves wonders if it would be as nice as swinging among Lincoln's stars.

Our city has many stars.

They are the people who work tirelessly and for no compensation other than the joy of making a difference in our community.

During the July 12 City Council meeting, Jeeves learned about Lincoln Hills Foundation from its secretary, Jean Ebenholtz.

During her presentation, Jean reminded council that no one in this nonprofit group receives any pay for all that it does.

Jeeves also learned about how much Lincoln Hills Foundation does for Lincoln on a citywide basis.

Since 2003, the foundation has distributed grants totaling more than $125,000.

Jeeves discovered that all grants have gone toward groups and agencies that assist and improve the lives of Lincoln's senior citizens.

Grant recipients have included Meals on Wheels, Alzheimer Caregivers' Support Group, St. Vincent de Paul Society plus many others.

The foundation raises money through the generosity of individuals, families, service clubs and businesses.

Additionally, Lincoln Hills Foundation raises money by selling "Dine and Shop Around Lincoln" coupon envelopes at $20 each.

Each envelope contains more than 120 coupons that represent an estimated value of more than $1,600.

Jeeves proudly purchased a coupon book by mailing $20 to Lincoln Hills Foundation, P.O. Box 220, Lincoln, CA 95648.

In addition to showing his support for Lincoln Hills Foundation, Jeeves is also showing his support for participating Lincoln businesses and restaurants.

He hopes that you will buy coupon envelopes too.

On July 12, Lincoln Hills Foundation presented a check in the amount of $1,500 to Friends of the Lincoln Library for the purpose of purchasing large-print books.

Friends of Lincoln Library is another group that works tirelessly for our community and no one receives any pay for what they do to make our city better.

Neither Lincoln Hills Foundation nor The Friends of Lincoln Library lose money.

Instead, they raise money to help make our city an even better place in which to live.

By doing so, they elevate us to even greater heights.

They are stars.

On Saturday, Aug. 6, Native Sons of the Golden West presents "Grand Homecoming Reunion Celebration 2011."

During this event, George Ahart, Aileen Gage, Evelyn Procissi and Herbert Hughes will be inducted into Lincoln High School's Hall of Fame.

They are also stars.

As it turns out, Jeeves doesn't have to fly to the moon to swing among the stars.

No, the brightest ones are right here in Lincoln.

Together with Jeeves, you can swing among them too.

🐾 IT'S TIME...

Jeeves enjoyed his vacation.

He is grateful to Lora Finnegan for filling in for him.

It was Jeeves' time for a break.

It is now time for him to return to work.

These references to time remind Jeeves of "To every thing there is a season."

Some associate these words with the lyrics from a song written by Pete Seeger and recorded by him, The Limeliters and The Bryds.

But most know that these words come from the Old Testament of the *Bible* under Ecclesiastes, Chapter 3:1-8.*

While Jeeves was on his break, he found time to read two books.

The first book Jeeves read is called *Verdict on Vichy: Power and Prejudice in the Vichy France Regime* by Michael Curtis.

This book is about France's Vichy government under Marshal Philippe Pétain's after its occupation by Nazi Germany during World War II.

The second book Jeeves read is called *The Last Lion: Winston Spencer Churchill: Defender of the Realm, 1940-1965* by William Manchester and Paul Reid.

This book is about Winston Churchill after he becomes Prime Minister of England and leads his country through World War II against Nazi Germany.

These are two different books about two different World War II leaders.

Pétain failed.

Churchill won.

While Jeeves was on his break, he also found time to read his emails.

One email included news about the resignation of Lincoln's City Manager Jim Estep.

Jeeves wasn't certain what to think about this resignation.

He remembers January 2011 when a petition to terminate City Manager Jim Estep and Assistant City Manager/Chief Financial Officer Anna Jatczak was presented to Lincoln City Council.

The council did not act on the petition nor did they terminate the City Manager and Assistant City Manager/CFO.

They stayed.

It wasn't time for them to go.

On February 25, 2013, Anna Jatczak resigned from her position as Lincoln's Assistant City Manager/CFO.

Anna Jatczak believed that it was time for her to go.

For weeks prior to his resignation, Jeeves heard rumors about the possibility of the city manager's departure.

These rumors may have resulted from several City Council meeting agendas that showed closed sessions with the City Manager regarding "performance review."

On July 8, 2014, Jim Estep resigned from his position as Lincoln's City Manager.

Jim Estep believed that it was time for him to go.

Jeeves has no idea why Jatczak or Estep resigned.

But, he does know that both thought it was time.

Now, it's time for Lincoln to search for a new city manager.

Just like the rest of us, Lincoln met its past financial difficulties with cuts in spending.

As City Manager, Jim Estep led the campaign to balance the city's budget.

This year, he presented a budget that he described as "consistent with last year's budget."

Based on current estimates Lincoln may, once again, face red ink in three years.

The new City Manager will have to lead that campaign to keep the city's budget balanced and in black ink rather than red.

But, Jeeves also believes that any city manager should be more than a budget balancer.

He expects more from a city manager than more of the same.

It is not difficult to preserve the status quo.

Pétain did and failed.

But, it is difficult to upset the status quo, fight for what you believe in and move forward.

Churchill did and won.

Jeeves believes that the job of city manager involves more than managing the city's money.

He believes that the job is equally about managing the city resources.

Some resources are tangible such as expanding the airport.

Some resources are intangible such as expanding ideas from committees like economic development

Jeeves wants someone who loves Lincoln as much as he does.

He wants someone who has a vision for our future.

He wants someone with creative ideas

Jeeves expects our city manager to be a stakeholder in our city.

So, he expects our city manager to live in Lincoln.

He expects the city manager to actively participate in community events.

He expects the city manager to regularly outreach to all parts of this city.

And, he expects the city manager to know more about the city's businesses than just what appears on the state's sales tax report.

Obviously, the candidate for city manager will have a proven track record from another city of comparable or larger size.

The new city manager should come to Lincoln with a complete understanding of our circumstances - good and bad.

Based on City of Lincoln homework, the candidate should also come with new ideas about how to attract new businesses, keep the ones we already have and get back the ones we have lost.

Jeeves knows that his expectations for city manager are high and they are tough.

But, these expectations are no more nor different from any corporation in the private sector would expect from its Chief Executive Officer.

And, Jeeves knows that the ideal candidate won't perceive these expectations as high nor will the ideal candidate perceive them as tough.

Instead, the right candidate will see City of Lincoln as full of opportunities that are worth fighting for to move this city forward.

To everything there is a season.

For Lincoln, Jeeves believes it's time for our new season to begin.

To every thing there is a season, and a time to every purpose under the heaven:

A time to be born, and a time to die; a time to plant, and a time to pluck up that which is planted;

A time to kill, and a time to heal; a time to break down, and a time to build up;

A time to weep, and a time to laugh; a time to mourn, and a time to dance;

A time to cast away stones, and a time to gather stones together; a time to embrace, and a time to refrain from embracing;

A time to get, and a time to lose; a time to keep, and a time to cast away;

A time to rend, and a time to sew; a time to keep silence, and a time to speak;

A time to love, and a time to hate; a time of war, and a time of peace.

🐾 FOUR-STARS...

Jeeves has been inspired.

He has been inspired by Michelle Howard.

Jeeves could hardly wait to tell the Downtown Dogs about her.

"Who is Michelle Howard?" asked the dogs. "And, why does she inspire you?"

"Michelle Howard is a U. S. Navy four-star Admiral" said Jeeves.

"We don't understand why she's inspiring or why she's important?" said the dogs. "After all, more than 200 other Naval Officers have achieved the rank of four-star Admiral since 1862."

Downtown Dog Luna recalled Admiral David Farragut.

"He was our nation's very first Admiral" she said. "He came to prominence during the Civil War. And, who could ever forget his famous command 'Damn the torpedoes, full speed ahead'."

Buster said "And, let's also remember Admirals William Leahy, Ernest King, Chester Nimitz and William "Bull' Halsey" who distinguished themselves during World War II and earned 5-stars.

"So, Jeeves, what makes Michelle Howard's achievement special?" all the dogs asked.

Jeeves sat up and replied "What makes her special is that she's our nation's first female four-star Admiral!"

She was promoted just a few weeks ago - July 1, 2014.

He informed the dogs that it wasn't until 1976 - more than 100 years after the Civil War and more than 30 years after World War II - that women were allowed to enter United States Naval Academy at Annapolis.

As a 1982 graduate of the U.S. Naval Academy, Admiral Michelle Howard has achieved many "firsts" during her naval career.

In addition to being the first African-American woman to achieve three star rank and four star rank in the U.S. Armed Forces, she is the first woman and African-American woman to achieve the rank of Admiral in the Navy.

Additionally, Michelle Howard was the first African-American woman to command a U.S. Navy ship, USS Rushmore.

In 2006, she was appointed Rear Admiral.

This made her the first admiral selected from her 1982 class and the first female graduate of the U.S. Naval Academy selected for flag rank.

Michelle Howard's accomplishments are so special that ABC Television named her person of the Week during it's July 4, 2014 broadcast.

And, that's not all she has accomplished.

Jeeves asked the Downtown Dogs how many of them had seen the movie called *Captain Phillips*.

All the dogs put up their paws and wagged their tails.

"Tom Hanks, who played the part of Captain Richard Phillips, is a great actor," said Buster.

Jeeves reminded the dogs that the movie was based on a true story.

"What you may not know is that Michelle Howard is a hero. She led the Indian Ocean multi-national anti-piracy task force and came up with the plan for Navy Seals to rescue Captain Phillips."

"Wow!" the dogs yelled in unison. "We now understand why she inspires you."

"But, why is she important to you and to us?" they asked.

"For me," Jeeves said, "Michelle Howard is a great role model. Although, we still have a long way to go, her upward movement through naval ranks more adequately reflects our society's diversity. She exemplifies what someone can accomplish if given equal opportunities to learn and to participate."

Alas, even though Admiral Michelle Howard has achieved great heights, Jeeves knows that she encountered many obstacles along the way.

She calls some of these obstacles "knuckleheads."

Despite the knuckleheads, Jeeves hopes that others will be inspired by Michelle Howard.

He hopes more, like her, who believed that they could not participate in the past, will seek higher office in the military, in business, in education and in government.

Jeeves hopes that after this year's elections, our federal, state and city governments will reflect our diversity in greater numbers than before.

He has reviewed City of Lincoln's last census results (censusviewer.com/city/CA/Lincoln).

The 2010 census reveals that females account for 51.94% of Lincoln's population.

Further, persons age 18 to 64 years account for 52.29%.

Whites account for 79.61%.

Hispanic or Latino Origin account for 17.74%.

The 2010 census reveals many more statistics all of which reflect Lincoln's diversity with respect to gender, age and ethnicity.

Jeeves is not suggesting that our city, or any government body, should reflect our diversity on a strictly percentage basis.

As always, he wants us to elect the best people to lead us.

But, Jeeves does hope that those who believe that they are qualified, like Michelle Howard, will step forward no matter where they find themselves listed in the census.

He does not want anyone to be inhibited from running for higher office because of perceptions based on the past.

Jeeves looks forward to four-star leaders.

To paraphrase our first Admiral and our most recent one, "Damn the knuckleheads, full speed ahead."

🐾 CARE, CUSTODY AND CONTROL...

Over the past two weeks, you may have noticed that Jeeves published a new email address, justinfromjeeves@gmail.com.

The first part of his address remains the name but the name of his service provider is different.

Jeeves now uses "gmail" as his Internet service provider in order to protect himself and others who may wish to contact him.

Recently, Jeeves' account with his former service provider was compromised.

Someone or some organization "hacked" into his account and made nefarious use of his address book.

Jeeves would have preferred to stay with his former service provider by using a different name and password combination.

He tried to make it work.

However, his service provider's reaction to his concerns over the breach in security forced him reconsider his relationship.

When Jeeves reported the problem to his former provider, it suggested that the fault was his.

His provider opined that Jeeves computer must have a contracted a computer virus.

A complete scan showed that no such virus had infiltrated his computer.

It wasn't Jeeves' fault after all.

Then, the provider recommended that he purchase insurance to protect his account against any future infiltrations.

This response, more than the other one, disturbed Jeeves.

Although he does not have much money, Jeeves makes deposits into a petty cash account at a local bank from time to time.

He has complete confidence that the bank will keep his money safe.

Jeeves does not have to supply his bank with armed guards.

Nor, does he have to purchase protection.

His bank is insured with the Federal Deposit Insurance Corporation.

Even, if the bank is robbed (perish the thought), Jeeves knows that when he goes to make a withdrawal his money will be available to him.

He trusts his bank.

Jeeves wishes he could trust his former Internet service provider to secure his information from thieves.

He believes that it is their responsibility to secure his account, not his.

Further, he believes that he should not have to pay an extra fee for such security.

Of course, Jeeves realizes that he must prudent with his Internet account.

For example, he doesn't share his password and tries to visit only secure websites.

Jeeves wonders why we have to keep paying to keep our identities safe.

Jeeves doesn't have a credit card nor does he have a debit card.

But, he understands that credit and debit card companies expect fees to protect cards they issue.

This does not make sense to Jeeves.

If they offer a convenience for which they are paid through transaction fees, Jeeves cannot understand paying twice for something they should already be doing on our behalf.

The general rule is that we purchase insurance for things in our care, custody and control.

For example, if we own a car, we usually insure it against loss or theft.

If we own a house, we usually insure for the same reasons

Jeeves believes that when service providers have our information in their care, custody and control, it is their responsibility to both insure and ensure its safety.

He is tired of being pursued to purchase insurance on items that are outside of his care, custody and control.

Jeeves will do all he can to protect his identity by following the golden rule.

He hopes that those who seek to handle his identity will do the same.

🐾 MUSIC TO HIS EARS...

Jeeves enjoys music.

He listens to CD's at home.

But, he listens to his I-Pawed in the car.

Jeeves is a fan of Heather Sullivan's music.

Her CD called *Lady Killers: Songs to Die For* is a favorite.

Jeeves likes Heather Sullivan's renditions of Petula Clark's "Downtown," Dionne Warwick's "Then Came You" and Bette Midler's "Wind Beneath My Wings."

He prefers her versions to theirs.

Jeeves can hear the lyrics when Heather Sullivan sings.

She has a velvety smooth voice.

And, she accompanies herself on piano.

Last Friday, Jeeves checked Facebook.

He discovered that Heather Sullivan was set to offer a live performance from Pogacha in Issaquah.

Until last week, Jeeves had never heard of Pogacha or Issaquah.

Alas, Jeeves has never been north of Yuba City.

As it turns out, Pogacha is a restaurant.

And, as it turns out, Issaquah is a town near Seattle, Washington.

Heather Sullivan's broadcast was available through Ustream.

Jeeves had never heard of Ustream.

As it turns out, Ustream is a website that allows members to broadcast live streaming video over the Internet.

Jeeves was surprised to discover that Ustream provides video streaming services to more than 80 million viewers and broadcasters.

At 8 p.m. on May 29, Jeeves became another viewer.

He turned up the volume on his computer and settled in to watch and hear Heather Sullivan sing.

Jeeves liked putting a face to her name.

Besides being a great vocalist, Heather Sullivan is pretty.

He also liked putting faces to the members of the band who accompanied her.

They're great musicians.

Jeeves was happy to learn that, last fall, Heather Sullivan issued a new CD.

The CD is called *Piano Girl*.

Jeeves did a Google search and found online sources where he could listen to tracks from the CD.

He also found a few sources where he could purchase it.

Monday, Jeeves decided to buy his CD through an online company called CD Baby (cdbaby.com).

The price through CD Baby was lower than other sources.

Until Monday, Jeeves had never heard of CD Baby.

As it turns out, CD Baby is located in Portland, Oregon.

CD Baby is an independent online music source.

It offers over three million tracks to browse, listen, and buy.

Sawyer Fredericks is another artist who can be found on CD Baby.

Fans of NBC's *The Voice* will recognize him as a winner.

After Jeeves placed his order, he received an email from CD Baby.

He was impressed by the timeliness of the response which included his order confirmation number, receipt and a postal service tracking number.

But, he was even more impressed by what followed in CD Baby's email to him.

It appears below in its entirety:

"Your CD has been gently taken from our CD Baby shelves with sterilized contamination-free gloves and placed onto a satin pillow.

A team of 50 employees inspected your CD and polished it to make sure it was in the best possible condition before mailing.

Our world-renowned packing specialist lit a local artisan candle and a hush fell over the crowd as he put your CD into the finest gold-lined box that money can buy.

We all had a wonderful celebration afterwards and the whole party marched down the street to the post office where the entire town of Portland waved "Bon Voyage!" to your package, on its way to you, in our private CD Baby jet on this day, June 1, 2015.

We hope you had a wonderful time shopping at CD Baby.

In commemoration, we have placed your picture on our wall as "Customer of the Year."

We're all exhausted but can't wait for you to come back to CDBABY.COM!!

Thank you, thank you, thank you!

Sigh...

We miss you already. We'll be right here at http://cdbaby.com/, patiently awaiting your return.

CD Baby

The little store with the best new independent music."

This email made Jeeves' tail wag.

He believes that it represents the best in marketing, customer service and promotion.

This email also makes him want to return to CD Baby's website to buy more music.

And, he will return.

Through CD Baby, he discovered more Heather Sullivan CD's that he will add to his collection.

If Jeeves can't go to Pogacha in Issaquah to see her, thanks to CD Baby, he can listen to Heather Sullivan on his I-Pawed.

For more information about Heather Sullivan, visit her website at www.heathersullivan.com.

🐾 BEST IN SHOW...

Most weekends, Jeeves is left alone for a few hours.

His family members go to movies.

Jeeves can't go with them.

Dogs aren't allowed in movie theaters unless they're service dogs.

Jeeves doesn't know why his family members leave home to watch movies.

He finds plenty of movies on television.

Since *Downton Abbey, Call the Midwife, Doc Martin* and *Foyle's War* wrapped up their seasons, Jeeves' family members tell him that there's nothing to watch on T.V.

Jeeves disagrees.

Besides movies, he finds plenty to watch on television.

He likes reality shows best.

Jeeves especially likes *Puppy Bowl* and *Too Cute* on Animal Planet.

But, his favorite reality T.V. show is the Lincoln City Council meeting.

This show occurs on the second and fourth Tuesday of every month except December.

Jeeves was disappointed to find no live broadcast of the May 27, 2014 city council meeting.

Thanks to technology, Jeeves watched the show via the Internet.

As usual, it was a great show.

The Downtown Dogs fail to understand Jeeves' fascination with the city council show.

Jeeves tells them that it's not enough to just read the council agenda.

Sometimes the agenda can fool you.

What may look like an innocuous item on the agenda, in reality, may turn out to be something much different.

Jeeves believes that it's important to tune in regularly.

Otherwise, it can be difficult to know the characters and their involvement in each plot twist.

Oh, Jeeves knows that the city council show is unlikely to win an Emmy award.

Yet, he finds city council and their exploits as captivating as any character or any plot line in *Downton Abbey*.

The May 27 episode of Lincoln city council was no exception.

If you relied solely on the script, you might be tempted to think that the show would be brief and uninteresting.

During Item 8.1 of the meeting's agenda, the city manager sought direction from city council with respect to subsidizing the 2014 Independence Day Fireworks Show.

Attached to the agenda was a Memorandum prepared by Confidential Secretary Pam Mathus for City Manager Jim Estep.

Both the agenda and the memorandum are available through the city's website.

The memorandum was clear and concise except for an omission.

This omission puzzled Jeeves.

And, the subsequent discussion, that took place between city council and city manager, was equally clear and concise except for another omission.

This omission also puzzled Jeeves.

Before Jeeves goes further, it is important for him to disclose that a member of his family has served on the 2014 Independence Day Fireworks Show committee.

This family member, like Jeeves, believes that the city should have a July 4 fireworks show.

And, Jeeves hopes that there will enough donations to adequately fund not only this year's fireworks display but provide a surplus for next year.

Any donations to the firework's fund are tax-exempt due to the committee's relationship to the Lincoln Community Foundation.

The foundation is ultimately responsible for the event.

Jeeves was happy to see city council come to a consensus about subsidizing the fireworks display.

Without sufficient funds, Lincoln Community Foundation could be on the hook for any shortfall.

However, Jeeves is puzzled over failures to disclose by the city manager and Councilman Stan Nader.

According to Lincoln Community Foundation's website, Pam Mathus is foundation Secretary and Councilman Stan Nader is a foundation board member.

Perhaps the city manger and Councilman assumed everyone already knew about these relationships when they discussed a possible city subsidy.

Or, perhaps because it was a city manager's request for direction rather than a vote.

Or, perhaps because the amount of money at stake was relatively small (up to $6,500.00).

Jeeves doesn't know.

That's why he's puzzled.

That's also why he's fascinated.

And, that's why Jeeves believes it's important to watch the show rather than rely on the agenda.

Sometimes, the script can fool you.

You never know what may transpire during the meeting.

Just when Jeeves thought the city's show couldn't get better - it did.

Under Item 8.2.b of the agenda, a Municipal Resources Group consultant made a presentation on Business Incentives.

The presentation was on behalf of the city's Economic Development Committee.

The purpose of incentives is to attract prospective businesses to Lincoln over other cities that, like us, are competing for new business.

The consultant reviewed other cities' incentives with our city council.

The consultant and the city's Economic Development Committee have been working on this project since last November.

Jeeves is puzzled why the city's Economic Development Committee would pay thousands of dollars to obtain information that could easily be obtained over the Internet or by making telephone call to each city on the list?

Or, why the city's Lincoln's Economic Development Committee would pay thousands of dollars for consulting services that offered nothing new or unique that might distinguish this city from our competitors?

Or, why did the city's Economic Development Committee take so long and pay so much to come up with so little?

Jeeves doesn't know.

That's why he's puzzled.

That's also why he's fascinated.

And, that's why Jeeves believes it's important to watch the show rather than rely on the agenda.

Sometimes the script can fool you.

You never know what may transpire during the meeting.

Just when Jeeves thought the city's show couldn't get any better - it did.

Under Item 10 of the agenda, Council Initiated Business, Councilman Peter Gilbert, once again, brought up the issue of plastic bags.

During a previous meeting, Gilbert asked the city attorney to research prospective state legislation regarding the use of plastic bags by retail stores.

According to Councilman Gilbert, the city has an opportunity to write its own ordinance.

As such, the city ordinance would take precedence over any state law.

Councilman Gilbert went out of his way, during two meetings, to make it clear that he was not taking a position one way or another.

Jeeves is puzzled why Councilman Gilbert, who claims he has no position on plastic bags, wants the city to develop an ordinance regulating their use?

Or, why Councilman Gilbert wants the city to do an end-run around the state's prospective legislation?

Or, why Councilman Gilbert wants divert the city attorney's attention away from important city business toward researching and developing an ordinance for which neither he nor other city Councilmen have any position?

Jeeves doesn't know.

That's why he's puzzled.

That's also why he's fascinated.

And, that's why Jeeves believes it's important to watch the show rather than rely on the agenda.

Sometimes, the script can fool you.

You never know what may transpire during the meeting.

Jeeves wonders why anyone would say that there's nothing on television.

He finds plenty to watch on T.V.

For Jeeves, the best show is the Lincoln City Council meeting.

🐾 THE WRITE STUFF...

Last week, Jeeves met with the Downtown Dogs around the fountain in Beermann Plaza.

The fountain is their favorite watering hole.

They like to think of their gatherings as being Lincoln's answer to The Algonquin Round Table.

The Algonquin Round Table started meeting in 1919 at the Algonquin Hotel in New York City. Also known as "The Vicious Circle," this group was comprised of well-known writers, critics, and actors.

Early members were Dorothy Parker, Alexander Woollcott, Robert Benchley and Edna Ferber.

Over the next eight to 10 years, the group expanded to include over 20 other members such as Harold Ross, who edited *The New Yorker,* plus sports writer Heywood Broun and actress Tallulah Bankhead.

Lincoln's Downtown Dogs form a much smaller group and are less noteworthy.

During their recent meeting, they spent most of their time talking about the demise of the typewriter.

Jeeves learned the world's last typewriter factory, Godrej & Boyce, closed.

Typewriters became obsolete when word processing became cheaper and more accessible by means of personal computers.

Nevertheless, both he and the dogs mourn the loss of an instrument that once played such an important part in our lives.

Although Jeeves owns a portable typewriter, he can't find ribbon for it.

So, he uses a laptop to compose his columns.

There's a very famous dog that used a typewriter.

This dog is known throughout the world and he is a creation of Charles Schulz.

His name is Snoopy.

Most of us recognize the image of Snoopy sitting on his dog house while he types "It was a dark and stormy night."

Jeeves wondered about other authors and what they used to write their novels, short stories, plays, poetry, screen plays and other works of art.

For example, what brand of typewriter did P.G. Wodehouse use to write about his namesake, the gentleman's gentleman known as Jeeves.

Jeeves discovered that "P.G." stands for Pelham Grenville and that Wodehouse used several brands of typewriters throughout his career.

First, he used a Monarch, then he used a 1940's Royal desktop and later, he is photographed using a Royal standard electric typewriter.

While doing his research, Jeeves also made some other discoveries.

The first typewriter patent was obtained in 1714 but typewriters did not gain greater acceptance until the 1860's.

Mark Twain purchased a Sholes & Glidden in 1874.

However, he completed most of his works in longhand.

But, Mark Twain is recognized as the first person to submit a novel, *Life on the Mississippi,* in typed form to his publisher.

The creator of James Bond 007, author Ian Fleming, used Royal portable typewriters and is reported to have owned a gold-plated one.

Similarly, Bing Crosby, Ernest Hemingway, Katharine Hepburn, Dashiel Hammett and Ring Lardner used different models of Royal typewriters at various times throughout their lives.

Hemingway also made use of an Underwood typewriter as did Carl Sandburg, Damon Runyon, Raymond Chandler, Earle Stanley Gardner, Sinclair Lewis, Carson McCullers, Jack Kerouac and Roy Orbison.

But, John Steinbeck used both a Hermes Baby and IBM while J.R.R. Tolkein used a Hammond and Jack London used a Standard Folding.

Jeeves has not yet been able to find out which brands of typewriters that the authors of The Algonquin Round Table may have used.

He did learn that Robert Benchley once said that "The biggest obstacle to professional writing is the necessity for changing a typewriter ribbon."

Now that the typewriter is becoming a relic of the past, Jeeves wonders what types of processors and software these authors would select if they were writing today.

Hemingway and Kerouac wouldn't need to worry about the weight of lugging a typewriter with them on their many different types of travels.

They could simply take a small disk with them in their shirt pockets.

This disk could hold all of their works in one space along with an entire dictionary and thesaurus plus spell and grammar checking software.

But, Jeeves continues to hold onto the romantic notion that they would prefer heavier equipment.

He believes that their typewriters were as much a part of them as their ideas.

Jeeves is reminded of a Dorothy Parker quotation.

She said, "There's a hell of a distance between wise-cracking and wit. Wit has truth in it; wise-cracking is simply calisthenics with words."

Jeeves believes that there an equally big distance between word processing and writing.

He deeply regrets the loss of something, albeit a heavy machine, that was so much an integral part of the twentieth century's best writings.

Jeeves is sure that if asked to use a word processor, Dorothy Parker would have said, once again, "You can't teach an old dogma new tricks."

🐾 PET PEEVE...

Jeeves is always happy to hear from readers.

Some contact him by email.

Some post comments on his website.

And, readers stop him on the street.

Some like what Jeeves posts on his blog.

Some don't like what Jeeves posts on his blog.

Some offer suggestions.

And, some ask questions.

Often, readers ask "when are you going to write about city council?"

They want to know what's going on.

For the record, Jeeves has no inside information about what goes on at city council.

What he does know, he learns by reading the city council agenda and by watching city council meetings.

Jeeves wishes that he had more to report about our city council.

Alas, he doesn't.

Yet, he should.

After all, the city council agenda for Tuesday, June 9 revealed at least 25 issues.

These issues involve millions of dollars in city expenditures.

One of the most important issues was Item 10. A which concerned City of Lincoln's Annual Budget and Capital Improvement Plan.

Jeeves was happy to learn from the city's Support Services Director Steve Ambrose that City of Lincoln has a balanced budget.

The budget also shows a surplus of about $223,000.

Due to Councilman Gabriel Hydrick's absence, city council voted to postpone approval of the budget until their next meeting June 23, 2015.

So, with so much on the city council agenda, why doesn't Jeeves have more to report?

Simply stated, it's because the city council offers so little that's new and different.

It's same old, same old.

For example, Economic Development Department had its hand out, again.

This time, it wants a piece of the surplus pie.

It has already spent tens of thousands on dollars on questionable systems, like Opsites.

It has already spent tens of thousands of dollars on a full-time director.

But, Jeeves can detect no results for all the money it has squandered.

As a result, he wonders about its direction.

Yet, Economic Development Department continues to believe that it's entitled to more money.

Fortunately, during Tuesday night's meeting, Councilman Spencer Short emphasized the importance of support for public safety.

He went on to explain that, when a community is safe, new business and residential development follow.

Councilman Short knows that business and residential development do not come to cities that are unsafe.

Some will point to the return of Taco Bell as an Economic Development Department accomplishment.

They will use it as their rationale for giving more to this department.

They're ill-advised.

Councilman Stan Nader, more than anyone else in our city government, is responsible for the return of Taco Bell to Lincoln,

And, Councilmen Nader and Short have come up with more ideas and more practical business development solutions than anyone in the city's Economic Development Department.

Ironically, neither Nader nor Short serve as city council's representatives on the Economic Development committee.

Instead, Mayor Paul Joiner and Councilman Peter Gilbert serve as this city's representatives.

So, how are they doing?

When he's not posing for photos as the face of Lincoln, Mayor Joiner seems content to rearrange the chairs for city council meetings and the images on the city corporate seal.

Despite what he posts on Facebook, Mayor Paul Joiner has little to show for his latest term in office.

During the May 5, 2015 State Resources Control Board meeting, through a Facebook post, Mayor Paul Joiner claimed that he was looking out for the city's interests.

Unfortunately, all he was doing was looking out for his interests.

Public Works Director Jennifer Hanson and Councilman Spencer Short addressed the board on City of Lincoln's behalf.

Mayor Joiner appears to be more interested in reelection than he is about the effect of the drought on our city.

He has a new Facebook page -https://www.facebook.com/PaulJoinerForLincolnCityCouncil.

It states "Believe it or not it's time to start planning for the 2016 Lincoln City Council elections!"

Really?

When Councilman Peter Gilbert is not reminding us about his past as a former banker and as a former Foster City Councilman, he continues to live in the past.

It's been 33 years since council member Gilbert served as a Foster City council member.

A lot has happened during that time.

For example, people now have cell phones, personal computers and tablets.

So, when Councilman Gilbert talks about the idea of a "white paper" to compile information on a specific issue, like water shortage, he doesn't seem to understand that people now obtain and retrieve data differently.

People obtain data from cyberspace.

And, they retrieve it in a nano second.

Councilman Gilbert seems unfamiliar with cyberspace.

Instead, Peter Gilbert often sounds as if he's in outer space.

If Jeeves seems like he's frustrated, that's because Jeeves is frustrated.

He is frustrated based on what he sees going on at city council meetings.

And, he is frustrated based on what he doesn't see going on at city council meetings.

Based on what Jeeves sees, Councilmen Stan Nader and Spencer Short represent 40% of city council yet they are doing all the heavy lifting.

Based on what Jeeves sees, Nader and Short:
- challenge city staff about their recommendations
- question consultants about their capabilities, fees and timetables
- make difficult decisions even when it means they must vote under protest or against other Councilmen
- take nothing for granted
- commit 100% to our city's issues
- use Facebook to advance City of Lincoln's interests not their own.

Unlike Mayor Joiner, Councilman Short has posted two columns about the water shortage on his Facebook page.

Councilman Gabriel Hydrick contributes too, but not as much as he could and should.

Too often, he wastes city council's time by speaking about his pet peeve, civil liberties.

Jeeves wonders why Councilman Hydrick doesn't run for state or federal office if civil liberties are his primary concern.

At the city government level, Jeeves believes that Councilmen, like Hydrick, should concern themselves with issues like police, fire, libraries, roads, sewers and water.

Even though Mayor Joiner and Councilman Gilbert represent 40% of city council, Jeeves doesn't see them doing anything substantive for this city on these or any other issues.

They seem to be taking us on a four-year ride that's marked by use of a rubber stamp.

Sadly, Jeeves may to have to wait for the results of the next election before he has a chance to regain his optimism about Lincoln's City Council.

During the next 17 months, he'll continue to watch and hope for change.

Meanwhile, Jeeves always looks forward to hearing from readers by email, by post or on the street.

Readers always make him happy even when they disagree with his point of view.

Jeeves hopes that they will continue to offer their comments and suggestions.

And, he hopes that they will continue to ask questions about city council.

But, Jeeves he hopes that they will understand if he has little to report.

🐾 WATCH WHERE YOU HANG YOUR LEASH...

When asked why they stay in hotels or motels rather than with family or friends, Jeeves often hears people say "so we can scratch where it itches."

Jeeves wonders why these people need to rent a room so they can scratch.

He also wonders why they itch.

Do they have fleas?

Jeeves also hears people say, "If you lie down with dogs, you'll get fleas."

Why do people blame dogs for their fleas?

Neither Jeeves nor the Downtown Dogs have fleas.

But, like people, they sometimes get an itch.

When that happens, Jeeves simply stops and scratches.

The other dogs do the same.

None are embarrassed to scratch.

None need to rent a room to scratch.

Of course, they have no money for a hotel room.

Nevertheless, they remain curious about all the interest in hotel rooms.

Why do people give up the comfort of their homes to pay for private places to scratch?

While reading page A14 of the June 2 *Lincoln News Messenger,* Jeeves discovered that there might be a way to find out.

Lincoln Area Chamber of Commerce offers a one-night free hotel room at a local resort for both renewals and new memberships.

Jeeves suggested to the Downtown Dogs that they form a business and join the chamber of commerce as a way of getting a free room.

After all, the Lincoln Area Chamber of Commerce and Lincoln Volunteer Center offices on F Street back on to Beermann Plaza where the dogs spend most of their free time.

And, when the weather is bad, Jeeves suggested that they might be able to take refuge inside those offices.

The dogs asked if Jeeves knew what is involved with starting a new business.

While they admired his enthusiasm, the dogs reminded Jeeves that he's a little dog without any business experience.

Then the dogs asked Jeeves what Lincoln Area Chamber of Commerce has to do with Lincoln Volunteer Center?

If they joined the chamber, would they have to commit to volunteer as well?

They also wondered what the membership benefits are other than a free hotel room and a possible place to hang their leashes during inclement weather.

With so many questions, the dogs decided to form a committee to find answers.

They promised to report back to Jeeves within a few days.

The dogs made some interesting discoveries.

Lincoln Area Chamber of Commerce's website (lincolnchamber.com) revealed that an annual membership would be about $275 for a group of their size.

That's a lot of bones for any dog to dig up.

The dogs also looked at federal income tax returns for both groups.

The most recent returns that they could find were for the fiscal years ending 2009 (guidestar.org).

The dogs discovered that both the chamber and volunteer center lost money in that year.

Lincoln Area Chamber of Commerce showed an annual loss of $34,846 or 24.6 percent of revenues.

Lincoln Volunteer Center showed an annual loss of $14,209 or 19.6 percent of revenues.

Fortunately, both organizations had other assets to offset their losses.

The dogs wondered how a nonprofit organization of area businesses could lose money when so much financial and other expertise is available from its members.

It was even more puzzling when the dogs discovered that this organization has low overhead.

The chamber pays $1 per year in rent to the city of Lincoln when other businesses would pay more than $15,000 per year for the same prime location.

The dogs also wondered how a nonprofit organization of volunteers could lose money when it depends on "volunteers."

By virtue of being housed with another nonprofit organization, it appears to pay no rent at all.

As to what one organization has to do with the other, the dogs finally discovered that both share one chief executive officer.

What the dogs found out made them growl.

The CEO for Lincoln Area Chamber of Commerce was paid $42,131 or 29.7 percent of revenue for that portion of the year in which he worked.

What the dogs found out next made them want to howl.

The same person, in his other position as CEO for Lincoln Volunteer Center, was paid $77,646 or 106.4 percent of revenues.

Total salary for both positions but paid to just this one person was $119,777.

The dogs don't understand how an organization that depends on volunteers can pay its chief executive more than it takes in.

And they also don't understand how the same person who worked 40 hours per week for the chamber of commerce gets paid so much at the other for what should amount to part-time work.

Yet, according to the form that he signed, he worked 40 hours per week at that one too.

But then they remembered that this is also a city that agreed to pay its chief executive, the city manager; more than $200,000 during the same period.

Based on what they learned, the dogs told Jeeves that they could not justify joining the chamber at this time.

They don't think it offers a good return on investment.

As to the free hotel room membership incentive, they contacted this resort and found that they could get a room for under $100 per night.

In their opinion, that's a much better investment, especially when it comes to getting a good scratch for where it itches.

For the time being, they told Jeeves that they'll hang their leashes elsewhere during bad weather.

And they caution Jeeves to be careful.

If he lies down with CEOs, he could get fleeced.

🐾 A LEAGUE OF THEIR OWN...

Jeeves is usually a happy little dog.

When he's happy, he wags his tail.

When he's unhappy, he sighs.

And, when he's angry, he growls.

Fortunately, Jeeves seldom has reason to sigh or to growl.

Recently, he sighed and growled.

June 6, Jeeves heard that City of Lincoln's Interim Economic Development Manager, Isabel Domeyko, continues to seek "market-rate" tenants for two city-owned properties.

June 11, she confirmed that the city wants tenants for the second floor of Old City Hall located at 640 Fifth Street.

And, she confirmed that the city wants tenants for the building located at 580 Sixth Street.

He can understand why the city wants to fill the second floor space on Fifth Street.

It's vacant.

The city has an opportunity to generate some additional revenue for unused space.

But, he can't understand why the city wants to take the Sixth Street space away from Art League of Lincoln.

It's full.

The notion of evicting Art League of Lincoln upset Jeeves to such an extent that he called a special meeting of all the dogs - Downtown Dogs, Neighborhood Dogs and Country Dogs.

Like Jeeves, the dogs wondered why the city would stop at two city-owned properties, especially if it needs revenue?

Why doesn't the city rent them all?

Or, why doesn't the city sell them all?

The city owns the building at 540 F Street.

It houses Lincoln Area Chamber of Commerce.

Why is it exempt?

The city also owns the first floor of the building at 640 Fifth Street

It houses the Lincoln Area Archives Museum.

Why is it exempt?

The city owns the building at 590 Fifth Street.

It houses the Carnegie Library.

Why is it exempt?

The city owns the building at 511 Fifth Street.

It houses the Civic Auditorium.

Why is it exempt?

The city owns the building at 2010 First Street.

It houses the Community Center.

Why is it exempt?

The city owns the building at 65 McBean Park Drive.

It houses McBean Pavilion.

Why is it exempt?

The city owns the building at 600 Sixth Street.

It houses City Hall.

Why is it exempt?

The dogs couldn't come with answers to these questions about these city-owned properties.

Nor could they come up with any reason why the city would want to pull space out from under Art League of Lincoln.

The dogs are afraid that Art League of Lincoln will be homeless.

Neighborhood Dog Molly sat up and lamented "I know what it's like to be homeless. It still causes me anxiety. That's why I am so grateful for my rescuers."

"Me too," said Neighborhood Dog Disney "what would we do without the kindness and care of strangers?"

"But, it's about more than providing food and shelter," replied Nasha, the Scottie. "It's also about nourishing minds and souls. That's why the arts are so important. They make us all well rounded. Can you imagine a world without Shakespeare, DaVinci, Mozart or Robert Frost? Or, can you imagine a world without theaters, galleries, opera houses and museums?"

The dogs yelped "That would be horrible! What can we do to help Art League of Lincoln?"

Billy, the Country Dog, got up and with Springer Spaniel authority said "I believe it's time for us to make some noise."

"Well, I am good at barking," said Jeeves.

"No, not that kind of noise," said Billy. "I mean the kind of noise that attracts positive attention. After all, we don't want to do anything that detracts from Art League of Lincoln."

"Then, how about nipping at the heels of the Economic Development Committee?" asked Downtown Dog Luna. "Let's take on the members of this committee who are intent on ousting Art League of Lincoln."

"No" said the other dogs. "If we start biting members, the committee could report us to animal control."

"That's funny" said Luna. "Economic Development Committee is already out of control."

Luna reminded the dogs that Art League of Lincoln is run by a group of volunteers..

Art League of Lincoln is a registered non profit organization with many members.

Luna also reminded the dogs that Art League of Lincoln regularly attracts hundreds of visitors to Downtown through its many events none of which interfere with other downtown businesses.

Art League of Lincoln also adheres to the Downtown Lincoln Marketing and Branding Strategy.

And, a few weeks ago, Art League of Lincoln recruited many new volunteers to paint the exterior of 580 Sixth Street.

The league added value to a city-owned property.

Sadly, Art League of Lincoln had to go to Roseville in order to mount America's ClayFest.

The dogs agreed that Art League of Lincoln has done more than any other group to enhance downtown Lincoln.

They also agreed that it's time for our city council to quit paying lip service to the arts.

It's time for our city council to give Art League of Lincoln a permanent home.

And, it's time for the dogs to make some noise.

They know that it's going to take a well-organized campaign to help Art League of Lincoln.

As a start, all the dogs will insist that their handlers call City of Lincoln at (916) 434-2400 and ask for Interim Economic Development Manager Isabel Domeyko to let her know the importance of a permanent home for Art League of Lincoln.

Next, the dogs are going will beg their handlers and friends to plead with city council to find Art League of Lincoln a bigger home - one that's also large enough to mount America's ClayFest.

How about City Hall? asked Disney. "Not much seems to be going on there anyway."

The dogs laughed out loud over Disney's jest.

"But, seriously" asked Billy "what about the Carnegie Library? I don't believe it's going to reopen due to costs. Don't you think it would be a great place for Art League of Lincoln?"

"What a great idea!" rejoiced the dogs. "As they say in advertising, the idea has legs - four legs. We need to make it happen!"

The dogs will spread the word.

They hope it will be easier to find rescuers for Art League of Lincoln than stray dogs.

The dogs know that they will also have to rely on the kindness and care of friends and strangers.

But, they believe in Lincoln.

They have hope.

And, Jeeves now has no reason to sigh or to growl.

He knew that the dogs would come up with solutions.

They always do.

Once again, Jeeves is a happy little dog.

But, his tail won't wag until Art League of Lincoln has a permanent home.

🐾 THINKIN' LINCOLN...

Jeeves went out of town June 6.

He found it difficult to leave - even for a day.

Jeeves prefers to spend his time in Lincoln.

He always finds plenty to keep him occupied.

June 6 was no exception.

The Ford Tri-Motor airplane was in town.

And, one family member had a ticket to ride in it.

Jeeves was tempted to buy a ticket too.

He suspects that the view of Lincoln is magnificent from hundreds of feet in the air.

And, he suspects that the chance to soar over Lincoln is a thrill especially in a 1929 vintage aircraft.

Jeeves will never know.

He's afraid of heights.

Jeeves doesn't board anything higher than his car seat.

He's content with the view of Lincoln from the back of his family's SUV.

Jeeves was invited to another June 6 event.

This event took place in Berkeley.

His friend Kathy Weiner invited him to attend *Bay Area Book Festival*.

Jeeves traveled to her home in Walnut Creek.

Together, they boarded a Bay Area Rapid Transit train.

They took it from Walnut Creek to MacArthur station.

There, they changed to another train that was bound for Berkeley.

Jeeves was thrilled to spend time with Kathy.

And, he was excited to ride the rails.

When they arrived in Berkeley, Kathy and Jeeves were treated to a wonderful sight.

There were thousands of people already there.

Many visitors brought their dogs too.

Bay Area Book Festival hosted over 300 authors plus publishers, writers' groups, outdoor stages, exhibits, merchandise and a "Library Temple" made of 50,000 books.

Admission was free.

Jeeves met representatives from the San Francisco Creative Writing Institute and Community of Writers of Squaw Valley.

He plans to go out of town, again.

July 7, Jeeves will go to Squaw Valley to hear writers such as Mark Childress and Ann Lamott read and discuss their work.

But, while they were at Bay Area Book Festival, Jeeves and Kathy had tickets to attend an author's event in Berkeley Public Library.

This event featured author Kate Schatz and illustrator Miriam Klein Stahl.

Kate Schatz read from her book called *Rad American Women A-Z*.

And Miriam Stahl explained how she came up with the illustrations for Kate's book.

Jeeves enjoyed hearing and meeting both Kate and Miriam.

And, he bought two copies of their book.

After meeting more authors and buying more books, Jeeves and Kathy joined another friend, Monique Muhlenkamp.

Monique attended the book festival as publishing representative for New World Library.

Together they enjoyed lunch at a French food restaurant on Shattuck Avenue.

Over lunch, they discussed book festivals.

Jeeves was surprised to discover that this was the inaugural *Bay Area Book Festival*.

Based on attendance, Jeeves believes that Berkeley's first book festival was a tremendous success.

From Monique he learned that other cities in the United States and throughout world offer book festivals.

For example, Toronto, Canada holds an annual event called *Word on the Street*.

Toronto's is a one day event that started in September 1990 as a small book and magazine event.

Today, it attracts over 200,000 visitors.

Twenty-five years later, *Word on the Street* has remained true to its original mandate: "to foster the awareness and appreciation if the written word in our culture, promote local artists, bring the people of Toronto together in a celebration of reading and champion literacy as an essential element of a healthy community."

Jeeves believes that this is a noble pursuit for any city of any size and any location.

Many cities across Canada now hold *Word on the Street* events on the same day.

Jeeves wondered if Lincoln could hold a book festival.

For many years, Lincoln was known for its annual RibFest and ItalianFest.

Both events attracted thousands of visitors to downtown Lincoln.

Why not a Lincoln book festival?

After all, Lincoln is home to many authors like Myrna Ericksen, Jeri Chase Ferris, Jim Robinson, Linda Bello Ruiz and Arloa Walter.

And, Sue Clark informs Jeeves that Poets Club of Lincoln has more than 150 members.

With so much literary talent, Jeeves believes that Lincoln could attract authors, poets, playwrights, publishers and visitors to come to town for a book festival.

Perhaps someone with a proven festival track record, like Jeff Greenberg, could be persuaded to help.

And, instead of outside food vendors, perhaps downtown restaurants could be persuaded to come up with special menu items for this event.

Maybe Buonarroti Ristorante could offer nonfiction enthusiasts an entree called "Real Picatta" and offer mystery enthusiasts an entree called "The Plot Chickens."

Maybe Simple Pleasures Restaurant and Catering could offer fiction enthusiasts a sandwich called "Chapter and Wurst" and offer poetry enthusiasts a desert treat called "Lemon Bards."

Maybe Tugboat could offer mystery writers an entree called "Something Fishy."

One of downtown Lincoln's regular events is the Food Truck Mob.

Once a month, food trucks roll in and out of town.

Once a year, Jeeves would like to invite writers, poets, playwrights and publishers to come to Lincoln.

He'd like our city to become known for events that broaden minds rather than bellies.

He'd like our city to become known as "thinkin' Lincoln" rather than "stinkin' Lincoln."

So, why not an annual book festival in downtown Lincoln?

Jeeves believes that many visitors would come.

And, be believes that they would bring their dogs too.

Even at ground level, the idea of a Lincoln book festival makes Jeeves' spirits soar.

🐾 THE LONG AND THE SHORT...

Jeeves watched last Tuesday night's (June 14) City Council meeting on cable televison with great interest.

He knew that our city Councilmen would have to make difficult decisions with respect to next year's budget.

Our new fiscal year starts on July 1 - eight days from today.

Jeeves remembers when the City Manager advised council that they could expect draconian budget cuts without new sources of revenue.

After the majority of voters rejected the utility users' tax last Nov. 2, Jeeves knew that there would be no new revenues.

Like the rest of us, the city was going to have to learn to live within its means.

As a result, Jeeves thought he also knew what to expect when he tuned in last Tuesday night.

He could expect severe budget cuts.

Against this backdrop, Jeeves was prepared to see the worst.

Any regular reader of this column knows that Jeeves is not always a fan of city management or City Council.

Jeeves calls 'em the way he sees 'em.

During the last City Council meeting, Jeeves observed actions that allowed him to form some different opinions.

After a brief time-out, the City Manager offered to develop yet another budget scenario to respond to public-safety concerns made that night.

Jeeves understands how much time and effort is required to develop new budgets especially this close to the July 1 deadline.

He appreciates both the City Manager's receptiveness and responsiveness plus his offer to crunch the numbers, one more time, to find the best possible solution for Lincoln.

But, a City Councilman impressed Jeeves more.

This one Councilman distinguished himself from the other four elected officials.

For a man with the surname "Short," Jeeves believes that Councilman Spencer Short was:

- long on expressing common sense
- long on explaining options
- long on identifying pros and cons for each
- long on demonstrating leadership
- long on showing maturity

- long on exhibiting patience, and
- long on living within our means.

Although Councilman Short deferred to the other Councilmen who wanted to see another annual budget projection, he was prepared to cast his vote last Tuesday.

Jeeves applauds his efforts and his decisiveness.

He also appreciated the measured reason that Short injected into the budget discussions, particularly about the potential for bankruptcy.

If only the other Councilmen were so reasoned.

Meeting after meeting, Jeeves hears Councilman Gabriel Hydrick allude to ideas but brings none forward.

Jeeves believes that it's time for the Hydrick honeymoon to end.

After six months in office, this City Councilman needs to become a full and equal partner in this polygamous marriage that we call a City Council.

Good and solid marriages depend on more than sweet nothings twice a month.

So far, that's all Jeeves has heard Councilman Hydrick deliver.

Stan "the plan" Nader has been marginally better by promoting fiscal sustainability.

He should be better than Hydrick.

He has prior City Council experience.

But he must know that his idea to create a plan for future fiscal sustainability does nothing to solve our budget crisis now.

During last week's meeting, Jeeves was flabbergasted to hear both Hydrick and Nader talk about how they hope to restore trust to City Council.

Such conceit.

Trust, like all other virtues, is earned.

Since elected, neither has done enough to put themselves on the plus side of the balance sheet with respect to trust nor have they brought forth new ideas that would solve the city's current financial crisis.

Jeeves is not sure what to make of the other two City Councilmen, Tom Cosgrove and Paul Joiner.

Their eagerness to wait for another budget scenario suggests unwillingness to accept what they know is inevitable, unwillingness to deal with the city's very serious financial issues and unwillingness to make difficult decisions.

As a result, they may find that voters show equal unwillingness to return them to office in 2012.

Ironically, the long and the short of last week's City Council meeting is they, like Hydrick and Nader, fell woefully short.

Short, on the other hand, went the distance for Lincoln.
For this week, Jeeves finds himself long on Short.
He stood taller than the rest.
Jeeves calls 'em the way he sees 'em.

🐾 LET 'EM EAT CAKE...

Jeeves looks forward to July 4.

Independence Day marks two important events.

First, we celebrate independence from Great Britain.

Second, we celebrate the birth of our nation.

On the fourth of July, our country will be 239 years old.

Jeeves wondered if there will be a birthday cake.

And, he wondered about the size of the cake.

After all, it would have to big enough to hold 239 candles.

He wondered who would blow out the candles.

Jeeves asked the Downtown Dogs.

The dogs knew about the July 4 pancake breakfast sponsored by the Native Sons and Daughters of the Golden West - Veterans Memorial Hall, 541 Fifth Street.

The dogs knew about the July 4 parade in Downtown Lincoln.

And, the dogs knew about the July 4 fireworks display scheduled for later in the day.

Alas, the dogs knew nothing about a July 4 birthday cake, its size or who might blow out the candles.

Jeeves was disappointed.

Although he likes all Lincoln's 4th of July festivities, Jeeves likes birthday cake as much, or more.

The Downtown Dogs suggested Jeeves find another source for birthday cake.

"If it's birthday cake you want on the July 4," they said "find a birthday party for a person rather than a birthday party for our country."

Jeeves heeded their advice.

He conducted a Google search to find people who celebrate their birthdays on July 4.

Jeeves found a long list of people.

The list includes playwright Neil Simon, singer Bill Withers, actress Gina Lollobrigida, television personality Geraldo Rivera and President Obama's daughter, Malia.

Jeeves believed that all will enjoy happy July 4 birthdays.

And, he believes that at least one or all will enjoy birthday cake.

But, with not much time left, Jeeves has yet to receive an invitation from Neil Simon or anyone else.

He despaired of getting birthday cake on July 4.

So, Jeeves met with the Downtown Dogs, again.

"Jeeves, Jeeves, Jeeves," the dogs said in unison "we meant that you should try to find people closer to home who celebrate their birthdays on July 4."

"That way, you'll have a better chance of knowing them and receiving an invitation."

"But, how will I find someone at this late date?" Jeeves asked.

Downtown Dog Luna stepped forward.

She told Jeeves to attend the July 4 pancake breakfast.

"If you go," Luna said "I am confident that you will have more than a 50/50 chance of finding someone who will have a July 4 birthday."

Luna went on to say, "your chances will improve if the crowd numbers 23, or more."

Jeeves scratched his head and wondered how Luna could speak with such authority.

"Haven't you heard of the birthday paradox?" asked Luna.

Jeeves and the other dogs shook their heads.

Although life in Lincoln can be paradoxical, especially during city council meetings, neither Jeeves nor the other dogs had heard of the birthday paradox.

"Please tell us about the birthday paradox," they begged Luna.

Luna told them that the birthday paradox is based on the probability that, in a group of people, at least two will have the same birthday.

Luna tried to explain the mathematical formula.

But, the dogs found it too complicated.

Nonetheless, Luna convinced them of its validity.

They learned that, if 23 people are together in a room, there's a 50% probability of two people sharing the same birth date.

And, they learned that, if 70 people are together in a room, there's a 99.9% probability of two people sharing the same birth date.

"So Jeeves," Luna said "if you go to the July 4 pancake breakfast, you're sure to find a crowd 70 or more people and, as such, you're almost 100% sure to find someone who has a July 4 birth date."

Jeeves was excited about his prospects.

He thanked Luna for explaining the birthday paradox.

He would attend the Native Sons and Daughters of the Golden West's pancake breakfast.

But, before the dogs left their meeting, Jeeves had another question.

"What's the probability of finding birthday cake on July 4?"he asked Luna.

"Your question presents another paradox," said Luna.

She explained to Jeeves that, although commonly served, birthday cake is not a certainty at a July 4 birthday party nor at a birthday party on any other day of the year.

And, Luna knew of no mathematical formula to predict the probability of birthday cake.

Jeeves was disappointed.

But, he continues to look forward to July 4.

He realizes that he may not find birthday cake.

But, thanks to Native Sons and Daughters of the Golden West, Jeeves will enjoy a pan cake.

🐾 WE THE PEOPLE...

Jeeves enjoys celebrating July 4.

He loves watching the parade in the morning.

And, he loves watching the fireworks in the evening.

Yet, July 4 means more to Jeeves than a parade and fireworks.

He knows that 238 years ago, this great country declared its independence from the Kingdom of Great Britain.

And, he knows that 227 years ago, this great country drafted its Constitution.

So, it's more important for Jeeves to celebrate our independence and our many freedoms.

Although Jeeves has a British pedigree, he was born in Lincoln.

He's proud to be an American dog.

While there's "We the people" as part of our Constitution, Jeeves discovered there's no "We the animals."

His life, like all other animals, depends on the goodwill of people.

Constitutional freedoms are not applicable to animals, despite breed or pedigree.

Unlike other animals, Jeeves enjoys one freedom each week.

Through this website, Jeeves enjoys freedom of speech.

Freedom of speech is guaranteed under the First Amendment of our Constitution.

Jeeves does not take this freedom for granted.

He takes it seriously.

Jeeves admires all people who take freedom of speech, and all our freedoms, seriously.

He especially admires people who attend city council meetings and speak during the "Citizens Addressing Council" part of the agenda.

Jeeves wishes that more people would attend city council meetings and address city council.

He learns a great deal about issues that might not otherwise receive attention.

Each citizen has up to five minutes to address city council on any item that is "NOT scheduled on the agenda."

During one recent meeting, Jeeves heard three citizens address city council.

Each spoke on a different topic.

One citizen spoke about a public safety issue.

She expressed concern over the risks to our city brought about by trains that carry hazardous chemicals.

Jeeves knows that many trains pass through Lincoln every day.

What would happen if a train carrying hazardous chemicals derailed in Lincoln?

He was happy that someone took time to express concern to our city council.

Acting City of Lincoln Fire Chief Mike Davis explained that our fire department has received training with respect to hazardous chemical emergencies.

And, he went on to explain that our fire department has policies, procedures and protocols in place so that it can effectively respond.

Jeeves is grateful to this citizen for raising an important public safety issue.

Her name is Jean Ebenholtz.

Another citizen spoke about a privacy and a safety issue.

He advised city council that Sun City Lincoln Hills has a drone.

Jeeves wondered how former army sergeant, former Foster City Councilman, former Wells Fargo employee, former Internet start-up investor, former Sun City Lincoln Hills board member and current City of Lincoln Councilman Peter Gilbert could be involved in a privacy and a safety issue.

Then, Jeeves discovered that this citizen was speaking about another type of drone.

He was expressing concern about the type of drone that is a pilotless aircraft, operated by remote control and equipped to take aerial photographs.

Until this individual spoke, Jeeves had not thought about how an unmanned aircraft could affect everyday life in Lincoln.

Jeeves is grateful to this citizen for raising these important privacy and public safety issues.

His name is Shelly Ebenholtz.

A third citizen spoke about our water shortage issue.

She expressed concern about the approval of new housing developments when the city has voluntary water restrictions due to the drought.

Jeeves has been vigilant about reducing his water consumption by at least 20%.

As a result, he no longer has a back lawn on which he can play.

Like this individual, Jeeves also wonders how the city will provide water to new homes when there may be insufficient supplies for current homes.

Jeeves is grateful to this citizen for raising this important water shortage issue.

Her name is Lena Labosky.

Some believe that citizen comments to city council do not make any difference.

Jeeves disagrees.

They make a difference to him.

And, he believes they make a difference to this city.

Jeeves remembers the name of a citizen who, over fours years ago, addressed city council.

He also remembers this citizen's issue.

And, he remembers most of what he said to city council.

Four years ago, this city faced a deficit.

Over 100 people attended the March 23, 2010 city council meeting.

It was a contentious meeting.

Many citizens stood up that night to express their concerns not only about the city's deficit but what caused it.

But, out of all the citizens who spoke, the one who Jeeves remembers most is the one who addressed city council by asking them to "stop feeding the beast and starve it if they didn't want the issue to continue growing out of control."

Jeeves was grateful to this citizen for expressing his concerns about our city's deficit and our city's spending

His name is Gabriel Hydrick.

And, Gabriel Hydrick now serves on Lincoln City Council as our Mayor where he continues to make a difference.

Based on all that he's seen and heard, Jeeves believes that Jean Ebenholtz, Shelly Ebenholtz, Lena Labosky and Gabriel Hydrick are citizens who take our First Amendment seriously.

As Jeeves celebrates July 4 by watching the parade and the fireworks, he will also celebrate them.

🐾 CONFUSION...

American Association of University Women (AAUW) recently held a big event.

The event was called *Caring is Fashionable*

It took place Saturday, March 10.

To make sure the event went off without a hitch, AAUW held rehearsals the day before.

Jeeves wondered why the event was called *Caring is Fashionable*.

He also wondered if caring is ever unfashionable

Then he learned that the title was a play on words.

The event was a fashion show to raise money to benefit American Cancer Society and fund scholarship programs.

Dogs don't know how to play on words.

They like to play on grass and other soft surfaces.

And, dogs don't know how to create events either - not even dog shows.

Events are a human invention.

And, Jeeves doesn't understand why humans need to rehearse.

Dogs live in the moment.

For them, when it's done, it's done.

They don't care about how well they perform.

From the end of his short leash, Jeeves has learned that humans are a complex breed.

Their thought processes and actions are difficult for him to discern.

When dogs disagree, they usually settle things by growling.

If there's further dissension, they bare their teeth.

Jeeves learned that humans not only deal with disagreements but they deal with undercurrents as well.

And, when situations get out of hand, they have intervention and crisis management programs.

Jeeves also learned that some humans even use substances, like drinks and drugs, to help them cope.

In Jeeves world, the strongest dog gets the toy when there's a tug-of-war.

There's no program to help them resolve disputes.

As to substance abuse, most dogs know that if they drink from puddles, they're likely to get sick.

Jeeves was also surprised to discover that happy human faces, do not always mean happy human lives.

There's more going on behind those smiles.

Sometimes, there's stress.

Sometimes, there's strain.

Sometimes, there's grief.

Sometimes, there's disappointment.

Sometimes, there's contentment.

For a scholarship winner who has four children, copes with a learning disability and attends school, there's stress.

For an event Co-Chair who had to contend with both the event and relocating her mother-in-law, there's strain.

For a model who just lost her father and committee member who lost her husband, there's grief.

For a missing guest who just had surgery and couldn't attend, there's disappointment.

And, for a ticket holder who overslept and missed it all, there's contentment.

In a room full of people, Jeeves discovered that there may be thousands of emotions - all running at the same time.

Some will be happy ones, some will be sad ones and lots will fall in between.

Jeeves wishes that smiles could always mean joy.

Unlike humans, dogs are more predictable.

Sometimes, they wag their tails.

Sometimes, they bark.

Sometimes, they growl.

Sometimes, they pant.

Sometimes, they roll over.

Sometimes, they mooch.

There's not much more in between.

There's no such thing as subtlety either

Jeeves always knows where he stands with dogs.

He will keep trying to learn more about humans.

Jeeves knows it will be difficult.

He wishes humans had tails.

Jeeves could watch how they wag them in order to decipher their moods.

But then he discovered that humans have tales to tell.

That's another one of those play-on-words that confuses him.

Like his friends in AAUW, Jeeves will continue to care.

For him, there's no confusion when it comes to caring.

It's always in fashion.

🐾 TAKING STOCK...

Jeeves' birthday is in April.

He will be 9 years old.

In people years, that's about 63 years old.

As each years passes, Jeeves takes stock of his life.

Based on what he sees on television, many people are taking stock of their lives too.

They frequent websites like ancestry.com and myheritage.com.

Some even have their DNA analyzed as a way of learning more about their past.

Jeeves has no interest in his DNA.

He worries more about the marks he leaves behind than any genetic markers.

Every week, Jeeves reads the obituaries.

Seldom does he recognize anyone.

But, when he does, it makes him sad to realize that someone will no longer be a part of our lives.

Jeeves is fascinated by the obituaries that include photographs.

Somehow, a photograph makes the obituary more meaningful to him.

He can put a face to a name.

Jeeves reads the obituaries not because he has a morbid curiosity.

Instead, he reads them because he has an interest in how these people led their lives and the legacies they have left behind.

Jeeves has discovered that each legacy is different.

Some times, it shaped by parents.

Some times, it is shaped by marriage.

Some times, it is shaped by children.

Some times, it is shaped by education.

Some times, it is shaped by military service.

Some times, it is shaped by career.

Some times, it is shaped by creativity.

Some times, it is shaped by volunteerism.

Some times, it is shaped by hardship.

But, more often, it's shaped by a combination of some or all of the above factors.

Jeeves can't remember reading about any life that was shaped by good luck although it may have played a part.

He especially likes obituaries that include two photographs - a youthful one and the other nearer the time of death.

Some people look almost the same despite the passage of time.

Yet, others have been transformed by the passage of time.

Jeeves takes his inspiration from the lives that they have led.

But, he takes greater inspiration from those who are still here and zestfully live in the world around them.

Two people who inspire Jeeves are Bonnie Dunlap and Estelle Feineman.

They are two women who are active participants in this world and who transform it.

Their presence among us makes every living day better than the day before.

Although both women are over 90 years old, their ages are incidental to the lives that they lead.

Despite the loss of their husbands, Hank and George, they continue to be fun-loving, humorous, energetic and joyful individuals who savor all that the world has to offer.

Jeeves is confident that they are more concerned with living their life to the fullest than they are with leaving behind any legacies or genetic markers.

In her characteristic good humor, Jeeves has heard Bonnie admit that she used to hide her age.

But, when she turned 90, she no longer kept it a secret.

Bonnie is an active community member.

And, no one, in Jeeves' opinion is better dressed or accessorized.

He knows many who, at half Bonnie's age, don't have half her spunk and spirit.

A few weeks ago, Jeeves learned about the extent of Bonnie's involvement in the Fine Arts Show.

Not only did she help set it up, but she was on hand to greet visitors during opening night.

And, Bonnie's involvement doesn't stop at fine art.

She's involved in many group activities including wearable art and antiques.

Bonnie designs and makes wearable art.

She also serves as emcee for the Wearable Art Fashion Show.

And, she continues to offer antique appraisals.

Jeeves knows that these activities are just a few of many that also include her children, grandchildren and great grandchildren

Estelle Feineman is also over 90.

When she turned 90, Jeeves asked Estelle for clues to her longevity.

In her characteristic good humor, she responded that she will live a long time because she has so much for which she has to atone.

Jeeves knows that Estelle was kidding him.

Because he also knows, first hand, that she is good and fine woman who could have very little, if anything, for which she has to make amends.

While most people would dread the thought of packing and moving to a new city, Estelle packed up and left Grass Valley for Lincoln to be closer to her family.

She was already in her late 80's when she made the move.

Right away, Estelle became involved in her new city.

She quickly made friends.

And, Estelle joined the Players' Group.

As a life master of the game, Estelle joined the legion of bridge players in Sun City.

From time to time, Jeeves has seen her at Beermann's on Wednesday evenings when her son-in-law Jerry McClendon plays as a "one man band."

Jeeves doesn't know everything there is to know about Estelle Feineman.

But, he does know that she participates in many activities that, like Bonnie, also include her children and her grandchildren.

Her daughter and granddaughters call her a "role model."

Jeeves calls her one too.

It would be tough to catch up with Bonnie and Estelle in order to find out all there is to know about them.

Both women are fast-paced and live their legacies.

Neither would stop to pat themselves on the back.

Even without testing, Jeeves knows that's not a part of their DNA.

Every day, Bonnie and Estelle leave indelible imprints that inspire him.

As a result, Jeeves doesn't need photographs to recognize them.

Like others, their lives may be shaped by many factors such as parents, marriage, children and education.

But, unlike others, Bonnie and Estelle have shaped the world around them.

As Jeeves takes stock of his life, he's happy to be pulled into their orbits.

🐾 R-E-S-P-E-C-T...

Late last week, Jeeves heard from his cousin Heather.

As you may recall, she had an unfortunate experience when she returned to the store and tried to pay for a television for which she had not been charged.

She was happy to report that when she re-visited the big box store, the Manager came running to not only thank Heather for her honesty but apologize for the untoward behavior of his staff.

Both Heather and Jeeves are happy that this manager displayed such good customer skills.

By example, he will instill such skills in his employees.

Jeeves wishes cousin Heather would come to Lincoln for another visit.

But, Heather has responsibilities that prevent her from traveling too far away from home.

Her mother is in an assisted-care facility.

As an only child, Heather believes that it is important for her to always be on hand, in case her mother has additional needs.

The care facility extends good care to her mother.

Heather tries to make sure of it through daily visits.

Recently, the care facility elected to undergo many changes in staff assignments, administration and events.

Adjusting to change can be difficult for anyone but it is particularly difficult for people who have been used to doing things a certain way for many, many years.

It is even more frustrating for people who have also experienced losses in their physical and mental well-being.

While change may be viewed as a positive for some, it may be viewed as a negative for others even when it occurs in a location familiar to them.

Heather has noticed that her mother is constantly agitated and out of sorts.

She is not alone.

Other residents seem equally unsettled.

Heather believes that these changes in behavior are directly attributable to all the changes occurring around them.

As her mother's advocate, Heather decided to approach the new director of care and discuss the impact of these changes.

Heather wishes that she could report more favorable results due to her meeting.

But, Heather came away being told that she would just have to respect their decisions.

Jeeves knows Heather well-enough to know that such a response was unacceptable.

Before she left her meeting, Heather took time to ask the director about the kind of respect that was expected.

Heather asked if the facility wanted "the Rodney Dangerfield kind, the Motown kind or the other kind?"

Jeeves didn't know that there were three kinds of respect.

Neither did the director of care.

Heather clarified each.

The "Rodney Dangerfield" type of respect is based on the comic routines of the famous comedian, Rodney Dangerfield.

This type of respect is the self-deprecating type that may elicit some attention, usually out of pity.

While this approach may have paid monetary dividends to Rodney Dangerfield, it offers no lasting value for the rest of us.

The "Motown" kind of respect is based on the Aretha Franklin lyrics from the song of the same name.

Those lyrics also include "sock it to me."

This kind of respect is the demand type that may also elicit some attention, maybe out of need and maybe out of fear.

And, while this approach may have paid monetary dividends to Aretha Franklin, it offers no lasting value to the rest of us.

The "other" kind of respect is based on the sum of many qualities many of which are intangible.

This kind of respect is the type that you earn and takes into account character traits such as honesty, integrity, reliability, commitment, consideration and more.

Like the other two approaches, this one may pay monetary dividends.

But, unlike the other two, this one has lasting value that transcends any financial gains.

It benefits us all.

In this ever changing and uncertain world, it's easy to become agitated and unsettled.

Sometimes it's difficult to know how to respond.

It's even more difficult to earn respect.

Heather respects the big-box store manager.

She's not sure yet about the new director of care.

Jeeves knows neither.

But, he does know one thing.

He respects cousin Heather.

She has earned it.

🐾 EYESORE...

Jeeves reads the *Sacramento Bee*.

And, he tries to read it on a daily basis.

Lately, he's discovered many letters to the editor about a particular issue.

This issue concerns Sacramento's recent purchase of an $8 million sculpture by Jeff Koons.

The sculpture is called *Coloring Book*.

It will stand outside Sacramento's new downtown arena.

Some letter writers support the purchase.

Other letter writers are against it.

On the heels of those letters, Jeeves also read a recent op-ed column by Karen Skelton, titled *Clean the blue trees, a blight on Sacramento* (*Sacramento Bee*, Opinion, Page A9, March 21, 2015).

Skelton opines about the Sacramento Tree Foundation, Sacramento Arts Commission, and Sacramento Convention and Visitor Bureau.

In 2012, this group paid $25 thousand to an artist to paint blue the bark on 20 sycamore trees.

After six months, these 13th Street trees were to shed their blue bark to make way for their usual brown bark.

It didn't happen after six months and still hasn't happened after more than two years.

The tree trunks are still blue.

Blue tree trunks upset Skelton.

They upset Jeeves too.

Like her, Jeeves doesn't like to harm a living entity even for the sake of art.

He wonders about three city organizations that were willing to part with $25 thousand to paint tree trunks.

And, he wonders about another city organization that is willing to part with $8 million for a sculpture.

For the record, Jeeves likes all types of art including some sculptures by Jeff Koons.

He likes some art better than others.

Jeeves wishes that he could afford to buy many types of art.

He knows that he wouldn't have to travel far.

Lincoln's art groups offer a variety of art at affordable prices.

Jeeves wonders why Sacramento's arbiters of art didn't make the 26-mile trip to Lincoln.

More importantly, Jeeves wonders why Sacramento's arbiters of art didn't look within its city limits?

Maybe they got lost in the blue trees.

Jeeves doesn't know.

Regardless, many writers, including Plato, William Shakespeare and Margaret Wolfe Hungerford, have paraphrased, "beauty lies in the eye of the beholder."

From time to time, Jeeves hears the issue of art in public places come before Lincoln's city council.

He also hears that City of Lincoln has no extra money.

When extra money comes in, it's sure to be slated for increases in police and fire department staff plus extend hours at our library before it goes toward art.

Just the same, Jeeves wonders what types of art Lincoln's city Councilmen would buy if they had the money and where they would buy it.

He hopes that our city Councilmen would look toward Lincoln's many art organizations such as Lincoln Hills Painters Club, The Lincoln Hills Photography Group and Art League of Lincoln for guidance and purchases.

He also hopes that whatever art they choose, Lincoln's city Councilmen would be mindful or our city's heritage.

For example, Jeeves hopes they would take into account our railway, ranching and farming history.

Without them, Jeeves doubts that Lincoln would be as it is today.

So, he hopes that our city Councilmen consult with Lincoln Area Archives Museum and other local historians.

Outside the Art League of Lincoln building at 580 6th Street, there's a large decorated sewer pipe.

Based on what he sees stockpiled on 7th Street, Jeeves assumes that the Art League sewer pipe came from Gladding McBean.

He doesn't know what the decoration on it means, if anything.

But, he believes that it looks out of place in downtown Lincoln in the same way the blue sycamore tree trunks look out of place in downtown Sacramento.

Yet, he also believes that some may like and applaud sewer pipe art.

After all, Gladding McBean has played an important part in Lincoln's past and its present.

Jeeves hopes that it plays an important part in Lincoln's future.

The May 2010 Gruen + Gruen *Market Analysis and Strategic Action Plan for Downtown Lincoln* report recommended using Gladding McBean terra cotta sculptures and planters to enhance downtown.

Jeeves believes that sculptures and planters would be great additions to downtown Lincoln.

But, even Jeeves' untrained eye can spot the differences between sculptures and sewer pipe.

And, his untrained eye can spot the differences between planters and sewer pipe.

Gladding McBean is referenced on pages 20, 30, 33 and 42 of the Gruen + Gruen report.

However, no where in the report could Jeeves find any references to sewer pipe, as art, for downtown Lincoln.

Despite the Art League of Lincoln's effort, he hopes no other organization seeks out sewer pipe art to form part of Lincoln's creative legacy.

No matter how it's painted or decorated, it's still sewer pipe.

Just as you can't make a silk purse out of a sow's ear, you can't make a Jeff Koons' sculpture out of sewer pipe.

Although many authors have paraphrased it, Jeeves couldn't find who first wrote "beauty lies in the eyes of the beholder."

He did find a celebrity, with a sow's ear, who added a new twist - Miss Piggy.

For Jeeves, she sums it up best.

According to Miss Piggy "Beauty is in the eye of the beholder and it may be necessary from time to time to give a stupid or misinformed beholder a black eye."

🐾 DESPITE IT ALL...

Jeeves regularly watches Lincoln City Council on cable television.

Last week was no exception.

During the public comments portion of the meeting, three audience members addressed City Council.

Two of these three express their comments at almost every council meeting.

Jeeves regularly expresses his comments in this column.

But, readers can turn the page or put the paper down if they don't like what he has to say.

And, they can share their dislike with other readers by means of letters to his editor.

City Councilmen do not have these luxuries.

They have to listen to all public comments regardless of substance, style or sentiment.

The third person, who spoke during last week's meeting, hails from Newcastle.

City Council listened to him too.

Jeeves is not sure why.

After all, he's from another city.

Yet, he often attends Lincoln City Council meetings

Nonetheless, Jeeves, like the City Councilmen, paid attention to the natter from Newcastle.

Jeeves was surprised by what he heard.

This visitor would prefer that the Lincoln City Councilmen hold off making any decisions with respect to "multi-year agreements" with city employees because of the upcoming election.

Jeeves wondered what would happen if our City Council stopped making decisions on this and all other issues between now and Nov. 6.

The Downtown Dogs suggested that City Council might look like our federal and state governments.

He wasn't sure what they meant until after he left the Downtown Dogs behind in Beermann Plaza.

Jeeves walked south on F Street until he came to Fifth Street where there are stop signs at each corner.

He saw cars come together at this intersection from four different directions.

Jeeves wondered what would happen if none of the drivers made a decision to move.

By watching, he determined that four lines of cars and trucks would eventually form.

Then traffic would back up and gridlock would ensue beyond the boundaries marked by this corner.

Jeeves now knew what the Downtown Dogs meant about our state and federal governments.

The Downtown Dogs see nothing but government gridlock.

Jeeves doesn't want to see gridlock come to Lincoln.

So, he's happy that our City Councilmen make decisions.

And, Jeeves was happy to hear Mayor Spencer Short say that he doesn't let the prospect of a pending election affect his decision to make decisions.

Maybe decisions are made differently in Newcastle.

Or, maybe they're not made at all.

Jeeves doesn't know.

Regardless, he sees no back-ups at the corner of F and Fifth Streets.

Cars and trucks move ahead without interference.

Jeeves hopes that we see our City Councilmen move ahead despite the natter from Newcastle.

🐾 TABLE FOR TWO...

Jeeves enjoys spring time.

It's not too hot.

And, it's not too cold.

The temperatures are just right.

Jeeves likes to frolic in the grass around the fountain in Beermann Plaza.

Sometimes, he'll roll in a patch of clover.

If he gets warm, Jeeves will stand on the edge of the fountain and wait for spray to waft over him.

It's more refreshing than a delta breeze.

From his perch on the fountain's ledge, Jeeves can see diners on the Simple Pleasures Restaurant patio.

He likes to watch while they enjoy steak sandwiches, salads, pies and many other treats.

Jeeves hopes to join them.

Thanks to an amendment to California's Health and Safety Code (Assembly Bill No. 1965), he may get the chance.

Effective January 1, 2015, state law allows pet dogs to accompany their handlers to outdoor dining areas.

Before he applied for a Diner's Club card or registered with www.opentable.com, Jeeves read the new state law from top to bottom.

He discovered that this new law, like other laws, has many provisions and exceptions.

For example, Jeeves discovered that this law lets local governing bodies, like towns and cities, to prohibit the presence of dogs in outdoor dining facilities.

So, Jeeves checked City of Lincoln Municipal Code (online content updated January 27, 2015) to see if any such restriction applies.

He focused on Title 5 which concerns Business Taxes, Licenses and Regulations, Title 6 which concerns Animals, and Title 8 which concerns Health and Safety.

Jeeves was surprised to discover Under Title 6 that the city manager is "the chief of animal control" (6.08.010).

He wondered if this provision is what Lincoln's city Councilmen use to attract city managers.

After all, the thrill of that kind of power could be intoxicating and could drive a man wild.

Jeeves also learned that, as of February 10, 2015, Lincoln residents are prohibited from feeding squirrels, rodents and wild animals on public property under Ordinance 895B.

Even though Jeeves suspects that he could be driven wild if he drank intoxicants, he's not categorized as a wild animal.

And, even though Jeeves is about same size as a squirrel and even some rodents, he's neither.

Based on his review of City of Lincoln's Municipal Code, Jeeves believes that it has no provisions that prevent him and other pet dogs from enjoying an al fresco dining experience.

Jeeves also discovered that the new state law prohibits live animals coming within 20 feet (6 meters) away from any mobile food facility, temporary food facility or certified farmers' market.

He's disappointed to learn that he still can't visit Lincoln's downtown farmers' market.

But he's happy to learn that the law prevents him from visiting a food truck.

Based on what they sniff after a downtown Food Mob event, neither Jeeves nor the Downtown Dogs wouldn't patronize a food truck anyway.

They support restaurants that are here to stay and contribute to this city.

They won't support food trucks that roll in and out and leave nothing but a smelly residue behind.

From his perch on the fountain's ledge, Jeeves can see just one restaurant that offers patio dining.

What if all Lincoln's pet dogs showed up at once?

Would he find a place to sit?

Do other restaurants offer patio dining too?

Jeeves had questions and he wanted answers.

So, he hitched a ride and took a tour of Lincoln.

Jeeves was delighted by what he found.

Besides Simple Pleasures Restaurant, he found the following restaurants have patios:
- Whistle Stop Café
- Beach Hut Deli
- Jamba Juice
- Crazy Sushi
- Meridians Restaurant
- Kilaga Springs Café
- Urbano's Mexican Grille
- Orchid Thai Cuisine

- Siino's Pizza Pasta Grill
- Waffle Farm
- Panda Express.

To be fair to these restaurants, Jeeves didn't check to see if pet dogs are permitted.

So, he recommends that all pet dogs ask when they call to make their reservations.

And, Jeeves doesn't claim that his list is a complete one.

He hopes that readers will let him know about other restaurants that he may have missed.

For the time being, Jeeves is impressed by both the number of restaurants that have patios and the wide range of cuisines that they offer.

They're enough to drive his taste buds wild.

This spring, when Jeeves sits down to dine al fresco, he looks forward to a meal that's not too hot and not too cold but just right.

Jeeves knows he'll find it in Lincoln.

🐾 MAKING THE GRADE...

Jeeves likes to ride in the car.

From his perch in the backseat, he can see other cars and the road ahead.

Some cars have bumper stickers.

Jeeves likes to read them.

Some are humorous.

Some are rude.

Some disparage our current president.

Some disparage our former president.

Some say "My son is an honor student."

Some say "My daughter is an honor student."

Jeeves saw one that said "If you can read this, thank a teacher."

In a few weeks, most students will go on to the next grade.

Thanks to teachers.

Many students will graduate.

Thanks to teachers.

And graduates will go on to enjoy bright futures.

Thanks to teachers.

Yet 25 teachers in Western Placer Unified School District face uncertain futures.

As reported in last week's *Lincoln News Messenger*, "Final Tally: 25 district teachers will be either be laid off or have their hours reduced next school year as part of an effort to cut $5.75 million from the 2012-13 fiscal budget."

The report goes on to say that "these cuts are being made to ensure the financial stability of the district."

Some of these teachers are sons.

Some of these teachers are daughters.

Some were honor students.

All set out to make a difference in the lives of other sons and daughters.

Jeeves wonders about their budgets.

He wonders who's going to ensure their financial stability.

Jeeves also wonders what their lay-offs are going to mean to students this year and the years to come.

Will lay-offs will mean fewer honor students?

Will lay-offs will mean fewer graduates?

Jeeves is certain that lay-offs will mean less bright futures for many.

But if you can read this, he hopes that you will thank a teacher.

🐾 WHAT PRICE BEAUTY...

Jeeves visits a groomer every four or five weeks.

His groomer gives him a bath, cuts his hair and trims his nails.

Some dog breeds, such as Labrador Retrievers, like water.

Other breeds, such as Yorkshire Terriers, detest water.

As a Yorkshire Terrier, Jeeves is no exception.

He doesn't like water and he doesn't like taking a bath.

But, he does like the way he feels and looks after his hair and nails have been cut.

So, a bath remains an inconvenience for comfort and good looks.

Now that Jeeves is middle aged, he wonders if it's time for a make over.

He's seen all kinds of television advertisements that extol the advantages of make overs.

Some make overs involve a new hair style.

Some make overs involve weight loss.

Some make overs involve different attire.

Jeeves has tried different hairstyles including the Schnauzer cut, the marine boot-camp cut, the long cut and the puppy cut.

He's settled on the puppy cut.

To Jeeves, no cut seems to make a big difference in his appearance.

But, he believes that the puppy cut makes him look more youthful.

So, his make over won't include a new hairstyle.

Jeeves weighs nearly 7 pounds.

He doesn't believe that he needs to lose weight to look better.

So, his make over won't include a diet either.

Jeeves picked up his new San Francisco 49'ers jacket last week at Fashion Fo Paws.

He now has his fall-winter wardrobe.

So, his make over won't include new clothes.

But, he wondered about other make over options?

Jeeves decided to consult with his pooch pals.

First, he contacted his French Poodle friend Cindy.

Even though she's a year older than Jeeves, Cindy has no need for a make over.

She's gorgeous.

"Mon cher Jeeves!" exclaimed Cindy "you are très beau as you are now."

Although he values Cindy's opinion, Jeeves decided to obtain a second one.

Next, he consulted Downtown Dog Luna.

She's also gorgeous.

And, Luna is often more objective and practical than Cindy.

Luna suggested that Jeeves consider cosmetic treatments for his make over.

"What types of treatment?" asked Jeeves.

Luna said "you may want to try dermabrasion if it's your face you're want to improve."

"What's that?" asked Jeeves.

Luna explained that it's like resurfacing streets.

It's going on in Sun City Lincoln Hills as part of a pavement improvement project.

Dermabrasion is a technique that uses a rough burr to remove and level the top layers of skin.

Jeeves was frightened by the thought of scraping layers off his skin.

Scratching behind his ear with his back paw is one thing, but the idea of skin scraping is quite another.

Jeeves reminded Luna that his face is covered in hair.

"Then," said Luna "maybe you should consider electrolysis."

"What's that?" asked Jeeves.

Luna explained that it's like getting rid of your lawn.

She reminded Jeeves that he saw it first hand when the grass in his back lawn was removed to make way for a more water efficient landscape.

Luna went on to explain the electrolysis is a technique that removes hair roots by means of electric current.

"But, because your coat is thicker than your lawn, it could take years to get rid of your hair," offered Luna.

Jeeves was frightened both by the thought of electric currents and by the thought of how much time it would take.

"Well, " said Luna "if you are looking to save time, maybe you should consider plastic surgery."

"What's that?" asked Jeeves "Except for my toys, I have no plastic!"

"Like you, Luna, I'm made of flesh, bones and hair."

Luna explained that plastic surgery is like reconstruction.

It's going on in downtown Lincoln as part of the city's 4-month multimillion dollar street scape project.

Plastic surgery is a medical procedure that reconstructs or repairs different parts of the body and sometimes includes transfer of tissue from one area to another.

It's just like the contractors who are taking jack hammers to break up downtown Lincoln's old sidewalks, lifting granite curbs and laying fresh concrete in their places.

Jeeves was frightened by the thought of anyone breaking or lifting anything on or off his face.

Luna reminded him that cosmetic procedures are usually worth the time, price and pain.

After all, Sun City streets will be smoother, your backyard will use less water and downtown Lincoln will be more pedestrian friendly.

"Maybe Jeeves," Luna opined "you're not ready for a make over. Why don't you wait for a few years?"

Alas, Jeeves agreed.

Instead, he'll continue to visit his groomer every four or five weeks.

The groomer will cut his hair and trim his nails.

He knows that he'll look and feel better after each visit.

And, Jeeves will now look at his bath water more favorably than he has in the past.

🐾 I LOVE YOU BUT...

During the Citizens Addressing the Council portion of the April 22, 2014 city council meeting, Jeeves was proud to see City Treasurer Terry Dorsey stand up and speak.

Jeeves admires all citizens who stand and address city council on issues that are important to them.

Dorsey spoke on behalf of Helena Chemical Company.

Helena wants to open a facility in Lincoln.

Initially, Dorsey became involved at the behest of a city employee.

Latterly, he became involved at the request of the company.

Like Dorsey, Jeeves knows how much Lincoln needs new business.

Based on what Jeeves heard, Helena stands to bring about $9 million in sales revenue.

That could mean about $675 thousand in sales tax revenue to the State of California and $90 thousand in sales tax revenue to City of Lincoln.

Jeeves encourages everyone to read about this story in the May 19, 2014 edition of the *Lincoln News Messenger,* "Chemical company looks to move in."

The story appears on the front and back pages of section A.

When Jeeves watched that council meeting more than three weeks ago, he was surprised by the reactions of city council and city staff.

At least one city council member said that this was the first he had heard it.

And, staff senior had admitted that they had just heard about it.

Twenty three days later Jeeves was surprised to read in the *Lincoln News Messenger* what city council and staff now have to say about Helena Chemical's entry into Lincoln.

Our city council would like this new business but "with reservations."

As the City Manager said "We're on board as long as they can do it in a safe manner. We'll do everything in our power to make sure they (Helena Chemical) can bring their business to town."

Jeeves believes council and he believes the city manager.

What troubles Jeeves is that they believe what they're saying is pro business.

And, that's part of the problem.

If Jeeves was looking to woo a prospective business, he would do it with unbridled enthusiasm.

His tail would wag a thousand wags.

For Jeeves, there would be no "reservations," or no "as long as."

Of course, he wouldn't allow an unsafe business to come to town.

He remembers the tanker fire.

So, it should go without saying that the city wouldn't allow an unsafe business either.

It's important to know that Helena Chemical primarily sells fertilizer to golf courses.

These are the same kind of fertilizers can be found at Lowe's or Home Depot.

Now Jeeves admits that Helena Chemical hasn't submitted a formal application to the city.

So, he can understand why the city council and city staff might be circumspect.

But, Jeeves would be doing all that is in his power to get Helena Chemical to sign on the dotted line.

He would make the effort to visit their plant in Chico.

Jeeves understands that any prospective new business relates better to a "how can we make this happen" approach than one characterized by exceptions and provisos.

So, Jeeves was curious to read the an adjoining column "How does Lincoln evaluate business." (*Lincoln News Messenger,* Section A, page A12).

He was surprised to read that "Each year, hundreds of new businesses contact the city with the intention to do business in Lincoln."

Jeeves wonders what happened to these hundreds of new businesses?

So, he sprinted over to Beermann Plaza and met with the Downtown Dogs around the fountain.

"I am surprised that we aren't gaining more business in Lincoln when there's so much interest?" Jeeves asked.

To which the dogs replied "why are you surprised?"

"Well," Jeeves said, "I thought that together with the city, the Economic Development Committee, Downtown Lincoln Business Association and Chamber of Commerce would be making a difference."

"Jeeves, Jeeves," they said, "their idea of economic development is to mount a monthly mob of food trucks on Fifth Street without any regard for the businesses that are already there."

"Jeeves, take a look at this city's track record!" the dogs barked

"Staples - going."

"Route 65 - going."

"Panera Bread - gone!"

"Famous Footwear - gone!"

"Chili's - gone!"

"Applebee's - gone!"

"Strings - gone!"

"Wendy's - gone!"

"Thai Basil - gone!"

"Beermann's Restaurant - gone!"

"And," the dogs sniped "there's one business that left and can't get back in."

"Which one is that?" Jeeves asked.

"Taco Bell!" they shouted in unison.

Jeeves reminded the dogs that other businesses have come in to fill some of the empty spots.

Family Dollar Store will soon occupy the space formerly held by Ace Hardware.

"Yes Jeeves," they said "but there's still a lot of empty retail space in Lincoln."

"And three businesses have come and gone within the least two years at just one location on Fifth Street."

Undeterred, Jeeves told the dogs how happy he was to hear Councilman Nader during the May 13, 2014 city council meeting.

Nader both pulled and voted against the Resolution 2014-080 to extend the Economic Development support Services Contract for Services with Municipal Resource Group.

"Yes," the dogs said "that was a good move on Nader's part. For that, we should throw him a bone."

"But, Jeeves," the dogs continued, "you also need to remember Nader's comments during the Council Committee Reports."

Nader said "we need to focus on exports rather than attracting new business."

"Export business indeed!" the dogs said.

"This city does nothing but export business to other cities."

This entire discussion left Jeeves despondent.

So he retreated to his bed to ponder the question of Lincoln's approach to economic development.

Jeeves has been around the block enough times to know that sweet nothings usually lead to nothing.

He believes that we need a new approach to woo new business.

Without it, Lincoln will be left at the altar while other cities honeymoon at our expense.

He loves this city without any reservations.

And Jeeves knows that with a new approach and better terms of endearment, others would stay and hundred more would come to fall in love with it too.

🐾 GLORY BOUND...

Jeeves woke up to see many U.S. flags in his neighborhood.

He likes to see the red and white stripes.

Jeeves knows that the stripes represent the 13 original British colonies that declared independence from Great Britain.

These colonies became the first states in our Union.

And, he likes to see the white stars against a blue background.

Jeeves knows that the stars represent the 50 states of our country.

He hears people call our flag "Old Glory."

And, he hears others call our flag "The Stars and Stripes."

Jeeves believes that our flag holds a special place in their hearts.

Our flag holds a special place in his heart too.

Jeeves knows that other countries, like Great Britain and France, have red, white and blue in their flags.

But, only the flag of the United States of America has meaning to Jeeves.

When he sees our flag, especially so many at once, it brings a lump to his throat.

Jeeves doesn't know why.

But, he does know that a special feeling overcomes him.

Jeeves wondered why he saw so many flags today.

So, he asked the Downtown Dogs if today is Flag Day.

"No Jeeves, " the dogs said "today is Memorial Day."

"Today, we honor Americans who have died in war."

They went on to explain to Jeeves that this holiday dates back almost 150 years.

Initially, Memorial Day was called Decoration Day.

According to the U.S. Department of Veterans Affairs, in 1868 Major General John A. Logan declared that Decoration Day should be observed on May 30.

General and Mrs. Ulysses S. Grant presided over the first large observance at Arlington National Cemetery.

Flowers were strewn on the graves of the Union and Confederate soldiers who died in the Civil War.

During their research, the Downtown Dogs discovered that observances were held in various locales - some before 1868.

Many cities in the north and in the south claimed to be the birthplace of Decoration Day or what we now call Memorial Day.

But, Waterloo, N.Y. was declared the "birthplace" of Memorial Day by Congress and President Lyndon B. Johnson in 1966.

Yet, it wasn't until 1971 that Memorial Day was declared a national holiday by an act of Congress.

The last Monday in May was set aside to honor those who have died not only in the Civil War but all American wars.

The dogs also discovered that about 5,000 attended the first ceremony at Arlington National Cemetery in 1868.

About the same number attend today.

And, they discovered that small American flags were placed on each grave then just as they are now.

In December 2000, Congress passed The National Moment of Remembrance Act.

The act encourages all Americans, wherever they are at 3 p.m. on Memorial Day, to pause for one minute of silence to honor those who died in service to the United States of America.

Jeeves and the Downtown Dogs will also take time out to show their respect.

They will honor the special men and women who sacrificed for our freedoms.

At 3 p.m., they will be silent as they salute them and our flag.

Jeeves now understands why it brings a lump to his throat.

🐾 OLD ELEPHANTS...

Jeeves stands in awe of Sacramento Mayor Kevin Johnson.

When most thought it was impossible, Mayor Johnson kept his city's professional basketball team, Sacramento Kings.

And when many others thought it was equally impossible, Mayor Johnson celebrated another win.

Last week, Sacramento City Council approved the construction of a new downtown arena.

Mayor Johnson exemplifies tenacious and ambitious leadership.

And, last month (April 16, 2014), those skills helped him become the 72nd President of the United States Conference of Mayors.

Jeeves enjoyed reading his inaugural speech (www.usmayors.org).

He hopes you will read it too because Mayor Johnson's speech is powerful.

In part, Mayor Johnson said "There could not be a better time to be at the helm of this organization because cities are back! Just a few years ago, in the midst of the economic recession, our metro areas were experiencing declining or flattening growth. Today, cities are pulling this country out of the recession, and Washington is beginning to take notice."

Jeeves doesn't know Mayor Johnson.

He wishes he did.

Jeeves would ask the Mayor to come to Lincoln and give us a pep talk.

Unlike other cities, Jeeves doesn't believe that City of Lincoln is "back."

While other cities are pulling out of the recession, Lincoln seems to be going the other way.

Jeeves admits that by cutting expenses, Lincoln saved itself from bankruptcy.

Our city council and city staff are to be commended for their efforts.

But, Lincoln does not seem to be moving forward through what Mayor Johnson identifies as "practical solutions, bold choices, and collaborative partnerships."

Jeeves can't figure out why.

Just after Jeeves posted last week's blog about businesses leaving Lincoln, he learned that Mimi's Restaurant is leaving Lincoln too.

Jeeves would like to post a win rather than another loss.

He would also like to see the same enthusiasm out of this city that it had from 2000 to 2006 when it was named by Forbes.com (July 17, 2007) as the fastest growing city in the United States.

Although Jeeves doesn't know Mayor Johnson, he does know another Mayor.

His name is Peter Robertson.

Robertson presided over the City of Brampton, Ontario.

It's a city that grew by leaps and bounds not only during his nine years as Mayor (1991-2000) but ever since.

Based on Brampton's economic development statistics for the period 1976 to 2011, the city has grown by an average of 12,000 people per year - from 100,000 to more than 530,000.

Brampton is now Canada's ninth largest city.

Yet, most people have never heard of Brampton unless you're fans of actor Alan Thicke or comedian Russell Peters.

It's their hometown.

While Robertson was Mayor, the city added 1,898 new businesses and 25,078 jobs.

By any standard, that's impressive.

But, why should Lincoln look at Brampton over other cities?

Like Lincoln, Brampton was founded in the 1850's coincident with the rail line.

Like Lincoln, Brampton is on a small waterway called the Etobicoke Creek.

Like Lincoln, Brampton started as an agricultural village supported by surrounding farms.

Like Lincoln, Brampton is within 25 miles of a major city and its state/provincial capital.

Like Lincoln, Brampton is within 25 miles of an international airport.

Like Lincoln, Brampton is within 15 miles of rail marshaling yards.

Like Lincoln, Brampton has a bypass around the city.

Like Lincoln, Brampton has struggled to maintain its downtown.

Like Lincoln, Brampton has experienced tremendous growth.

Unlike Lincoln, Brampton has managed to sustain it.

Jeeves wrote to former Mayor Robertson and asked if he would be willing to share some economic development ideas.

He was overjoyed when Robertson wrote back with a list of six points for economic development.

At the top of his list, Robertson wrote "If you bought it, a truck brought it."

He then went on to explain that manufacturing goods and food products need to be moved to market.

As a result, economic development follows highways and arterial roads which create industrial and commercial centers.

So, for Lincoln, any road frontage along our bypass should have industrial and/or commercial zoning.

In his words, "residential growth is wasted along major highways and interchanges."

Robertson began his second point with, "Old elephants need to go."

Jeeves wasn't sure what Robertson meant by this statement.

Does he think Lincoln has a zoo?

No, instead Robertson meant that office sector development represents a richer source of economic development than traditional manufacturing development.

Mid-rise buildings that incorporate commercial with residential uses make for "liveable/walkable lifestyle communities."

Thirdly, Robertson's wrote, "H.A.C.E. Districts have economic potential, big-time!"

What are H.A.C.E. districts Jeeves wondered?

As it turns out, H.A.C.E. stands for Historic, Arts, Culture and Entertainment districts.

Robertson points outs, these districts "like Yorkville, the Distillery District in Toronto, Soho in New York and London, or the urban core of Downtown Brampton, are rich if preserved with their existing urban architecture."

He believes that "an old town creates a character, soul and heart of a community."

Fourthly, Robertson wrote "a railway marshaling yard or container terminal for the interface of truck and is rail is magnificent for economic development, just as the land around an existing airport creates a venue to host businesses."

For his next economic development idea, Robertson suggests attracting a college or university.

Besides "the vibrancy that young people bring to a community life," Robertson has seen additional business outgrowth in the form of pubs, restaurants and residential housing.

Lastly, Robertson believes that "Waterfront development or a river walk are priceless in developing retail and tourism."

In addition to San Antonio, Calgary and Seoul, which he views as prime examples of a river walk, Robertson references Chicago's waterfront as "a classic example of how to preserve the natural features while adding a museum, aquarium, wharf and parks without spoiling it with high rise condos."

Jeeves is grateful for the time that former Mayor Robertson spent pulling together his list of ideas for economic development.

It's a formidable list.

But, as Sacramento Mayor Kevin Johnson said in his April 16th speech "Mayors are moving our country forward through practical solutions, bold choices, and collaborative partnerships."

Jeeves believes that Lincoln can move forward too.

But, maybe some "old elephants need to go."

🐾 SUBPLOT...

Jeeves considers all comments that readers post to his weekly blogs.

He enjoys them.

Jeeves always learns something new from readers.

They inspire him to write more.

And, they inspire him to do better.

Last week was no exception.

Three readers took time out from their busy schedules to post comments.

Jeeves is grateful to Jeri Chase Ferris, Shirley Russell and Fran Neves.

Shirley Russell's comments about the beginning of the First and O Street cemetery made Jeeves consider cemeteries.

Shirley indicated that this Lincoln cemetery designates areas for women and masons.

Jeeves wonders if this cemetery designates a place for pets.

Together with their estate planning attorney, Jeeves' handlers provided for him when they die.

But, Jeeves has not planned for himself when he dies.

He doesn't like to contemplate his demise.

Yet, Jeeves knows that like life and living, death and dying are realities.

So, he wants to have a burial plan in place.

Jeeves wonders how and where he will be laid to rest.

He checked the Internet and was surprised by what he found.

Within a short driving distance of his home, Jeeves discovered four pet burial firms - three in Sacramento and one in Pleasant Grove.

This discovery comforted him.

But, he was intrigued by pet cemeteries in other parts of the United States and in other parts of the world.

In as much as Jeeves has ventured no more than 100 miles from Lincoln, the prospect of distant travel, even in death, appeals to him.

Jeeves discovered that America's oldest and largest pet cemetery can be found in Hartsdale, NY.

This cemetery dates back to 1896 and serves as the final resting place for over 70,000 pets.

He also discovered the Los Angeles Pet Memorial Park and Crematorium.

This cemetery dates back to 1928 and serves as the final resting place for 40,000 pets including Hopalong Cassidy's horse, Topper.

If Jeeves has to go, either would suffice.

That was before he discovered three pet cemeteries in Europe and one in the Middle East.

The thought of being buried in London, England's Hyde Park near the Royal Marines Mascot dog, Prince, appeals to Jeeves.

The thought of being buried in Ashkelon, Israel, which is the largest dog cemetery in the ancient world, appeals to Jeeves.

And, the thought of being buried Venice, Italy alongside Peggy Guggenheim's dogs on the art museum grounds that bear her name, appeals to Jeeves.

Alas, these cemeteries are unavailable to him.

Then, Jeeves discovered Le Cimetière des Chiens et Autres Animaux Domestique in Paris, France.

Since 1899, this cemetery has welcomed cats, horses, sheep, hens, at least one monkey and many dogs.

The thought of being buried near the famous German Shepherd, Rin Tin Tin, appeals to Jeeves.

But, Jeeves wonders how he would get there and how he would pay for his burial.

After all, Paris, France is a long way from Lincoln, California.

Jeeves recognizes that he needs to consult his own attorney to help him make his final arrangements.

He'll need an expert who specializes in pet estates, wills and trusts.

Meanwhile, Jeeves will ask Shirley Russell to help him find out if there's room for him at the corner of First and O Streets.

# NO MAN, NO DOG…

In 1624, poet John Donne wrote "No man is an island, Entire of itself, Every man is a piece of the continent, A part of the main."

No dog is an island either.

And, regardless of how many holes he digs, or how many bones he buries, Jeeves has learned that he is just a very little piece of this great big world.

More importantly, Jeeves has learned that friends matter.

And, most importantly, Jeeves has learned that he must let friends know how much they matter.

Jeeves is just a little dog on a short leash.

From the end of his leash, he tries to spend every day in Downtown Lincoln.

Jeeves loves downtown.

And, he loves meeting the Downtown Dogs around the fountain in Beermann Plaza.

He sees them often.

Together, they debate local issues.

Some debates generate howls and moans.

Other debates generate growls and groans.

But, most generate lively discussion and tail wags.

He is grateful for his friends from around the fountain.

The Downtown Dogs inspire Jeeves.

Each one matters to him.

And, Jeeves is equally grateful for friends from beyond the fountain.

Over three years ago, Jeff Greenberg came up with the idea for this website.

It was a good idea.

Yet, Jeeves didn't do anything about it.

Instead, it took an offhand comment, by another friend, to spur Jeeves into action.

Several weeks ago, when Arloa Walter asked when he might return to writing, Jeeves said "I'm thinking about starting a website to post my columns."

Arloa Walter said "I wish you would."

She said no more and she said no less.

Yet, that's all it took to make Jeeves do in three weeks what he had put off for over three years.

Since then, Jeeves has wondered why Arloa's words inspired him to act more than others.

Of course, he likes and respects Arloa.

He values her opinion as both as a person and an author.

As an author, Arloa has presented opportunities for others, who might not otherwise be heard, to express their opinions.

In her first book titled, *Voices of Older Women: What They Want To Say… Why You're Not Listening,* Arloa gave older women a voice.

Now, in her latest book titled *Men's Point of View: A Snapshot In Time,* she gave older men a voice.

Jeeves realized that, just as Arloa inspired other to express their views, she inspired him to express his views.

Jeeves is grateful to Arloa.

Arloa Walter matters to him.

Once the website was up and running, Jeeves had to come up with columns.

Happily, that challenge was an easy one to overcome.

A more difficult challenge was finding someone to review them.

The Downtown Dogs offered to help.

While they're good at math, they're lousy at spelling and grammar.

And, the dogs didn't want the responsibility of checking facts.

Jeeves is grateful that Therese Adams also offered to help.

Therese reviews each column before Jeeves posts it on this website.

She makes sure that Jeeves can get out of the holes he digs and that he can find the bones he's buried.

It's no easy task.

But, Therese Adams makes it seem easy.

Despite her very busy schedule as an attorney at Adams Hayes Law, Therese makes time for Jeeves.

He is overwhelmed by her commitment, her advice and the depth of her support.

Jeeves couldn't pursue *Just in from Jeeves* without her.

Jeeves is grateful to Therese.

Therese Adams matters to him.

Now that Jeeves posts columns to this website, he has received public comments and private emails for many readers

He is surprised by the number of responses.

Each one inspires Jeeves.
He is grateful for your support.
Jeeves couldn't continue without you.
You matter to him.
Jeeves is no island, entire of himself.

🐾 FAIRY TAILS...

Jeeves' favorite rhyme is "Hey Diddle Diddle."

For those few who may not be familiar with this rhyme, it follows:

"Hey diddle diddle

The cat played the fiddle

The cow jumped over the moon

The little dog laughed to see such sport

And, the dish ran away with the spoon."

Some Downtown Dogs, especially the bigger ones, believe that Jeeves likes this rhyme because of the reference to the little dog.

He admits that he enjoys this reference.

But, that's not the real reason he likes "Hey Diddle Diddle."

Other dogs believe that Jeeves likes it because it is associated with Mother Goose.

They know Jeeves is a huge fan of Mother Goose on the Loose which is held Thursday mornings in Twelve Bridges Library until June 30.

Those dogs may be onto something.

Jeeves does believe that Mother Goose on Loose is the best children's program that Lincoln offers.

Because of the budget shortfall and uncertainties with respect to both libraries, this very valuable program has been threatened.

Jeeves believes that there are many adults, especially some in city leadership positions, who could gain a great deal by attending Mother Goose on the Loose.

Like Lincoln's pre-schoolers, they might learn how to listen, take turns, play with others, follow directions, identify new shapes and colors and show appreciation.

These skills are what Mother Goose on the Loose is all about.

Jeeves understands that Mother Goose on the Loose is available to City Council.

Our city leaders could learn more about what their libraries have to offer.

They could also find out what Lincoln's children like and why the program attracts so much community support.

And, most importantly, they could learn more about how to show appreciation for the many good ideas and suggestions that come from Lincoln's concerned and informed citizens.

But, it's not the little dog reference nor the Mother Goose connection that make Jeeves recite "Hey Diddle Diddle."

There's a simpler reason.

It reminds him to laugh when he might otherwise cry or turn on his tail and run.

Jeeves recites this rhyme every couple of weeks, usually during evenings on the second and fourth Tuesday of the month while he watches City Council meetings on cable channel 18.

And, sometimes he recites it on Thursdays after he reads the *Lincoln News Messenger*.

It helps Jeeves cope with hypocrisy that seems to be in over-abundant supply.

Jeeves is troubled by three recent examples.

The first example comes from a member who serves on the committee that has been asked to create a Request for Proposal regarding ways to ensure our city's future fiscal sustainability.

In a recent newspaper article (*Los Angeles Times*, April 28, 2011), he bragged about buying two new computers in Roseville and regularly dining there.

Lincoln needs all the tax revenue it can get to help the city become more fiscally sound.

Could this committee member tell us how shopping and dining in another city helps the City of Lincoln achieve greater fiscal sustainability?

Did the cat just play the fiddle?

The second example comes from a City Councilman who accuses a resident of throwing "bombs" rather than offering solutions (*Lincoln News Messenger*, May 5, 2011).

Could this Councilman tell us how his immaturity, petulance and incendiary language further constructive dialogue with the citizens he is supposed to represent?

Did the cow just jump over the moon?

And, the third example comes from Lincoln's youngest and most junior City Councilman who wrote a letter to the *Lincoln News Messenger*'s editor and suggested a tax (May, 19, 2011).

Could this Councilman tell us how he could base his election campaign as being against the utility tax (*Lincoln News Messenger*, October 20, 2010) and then turnaround and suggest a tax now that he holds office?

What happened to his election promise to offer "creative and proactive" solutions to our city's problems (*Lincoln News Messenger*, October 28, 2010)

Did the dish just run away with the spoon?

The Downtown, Neighborhood and Country Dogs tell Jeeves that he should start reciting "Humpty Dumpty."

They can hardly wait until the next city elections.

The Dogs believe that there's bound to be a great fall.

And, insomuch as Lincoln has no king's horses and Lincoln has no king's men, they hope Mother Goose is still on the Loose.

🐾 NOT IN VAIN...

Jeeves is sad.

He mourns the loss of a Sacramento County Deputy Sheriff.

His name is Danny Oliver.

He mourns the loss of a Placer County Deputy Sheriff.

His name is Michael Davis.

And, he mourns the loss of a Canadian reserve soldier.

His name is Nathan Cirillo.

All were killed while on duty.

Their duty was to serve and to protect us.

Last Tuesday (October 28, 2014) Jeeves watched the funeral for Cpl. Cirillo.

Nathan Cirillo was gunned down October 22, 2014 while standing guard at the National War Monument in Ottawa.

Ottawa is Canada's capital city.

Thousands stood along highways to watch the 323-mile transport of Cpl. Cirillo's body from Ottawa to Hamilton, Ontario - his home.

More than 4,500 military, police and emergency personnel formed Cpl. Cirillo's regimental funeral procession.

And many more thousands stood, three deep, along the processional route - quietly and motionless.

Their tears flowed freely.

The three hour procession and funeral were televised across Canada without any commercial interruptions.

Canada's Prime Minister Stephen Harper attended the funeral.

Queen Elizabeth II sent condolences.

During the funeral service, Major the Reverend Canon Rob Fead said that "Cpl. Nathan Cirillo's death was not in vain. Our country is more resolute, more unified and more determined to be a place of freedom, hope and peace regardless of race, language or creed."

All of these are a testament to the life of Cpl. Nathan Cirillo and to the regard that Canadians have for their soldiers.

As Jeeves writes this, the funerals for Deputies Oliver and Davis have yet to occur.

Deputy Danny Oliver's funeral will be held Monday, November 3, 2014 in Roseville.

Deputy Michael Davis' funeral will be held Tuesday, November 4, 2014 in Roseville.

Jeeves knows that thousands will also pay their respects to these men.

Their funerals will be testaments to the lives of Deputy Oliver and Deputy Davis and to the regard that Americans have for those who protect them.

Jeeves knows that their deaths will not be in vain.

We will remember them just as we remember our soldiers.

November 11 is an important day.

In Canada and Great Britain, November 11 is called Remembrance Day.

In the United States, November 11 is called Veterans Day.

It's the day that we that honor all those who have served in the U.S. Armed Forces.

In 1919, President Woodrow Wilson first proclaimed November 11 as Armistice Day,

In proclaiming Armistice Day, he said "To us in America, the reflections of Armistice Day will be filled with solemn pride in the heroism of those who died in the country's service and with gratitude for the victory, both because of the thing from which it has freed us and because of the opportunity it has given America to show her sympathy with peace and justice in the councils of the nations."

Tuesday, November 11, Jeeves will take time to honor all who served in our armed forces.

He knows that others will take time too.

Many will attend the 11 a.m. service in front of Veterans Memorial Hall, 541 Fifth Street in downtown Lincoln.

Jeeves will remember our veterans.

He will remember Cpl. Nathan Cirillo.

He will remember Deputy Sheriff Danny Oliver.

He will remember Deputy Sheriff Michael Davis.

His tears will flow freely.

🐾 AUDITIONS...

Jeeves enjoys November.

He looks forward to Thanksgiving Day.

It's a special day.

Like most, Jeeves takes time out to give thanks.

He has a great deal for which he is thankful.

Jeeves wishes that everyone could enjoy the holiday in the same way.

But he knows that many cannot because of difficult financial or other circumstances.

And he's sorry for their misfortune.

Jeeves also hopes that, between now and next Thanksgiving, their situations improve.

To the extent that he can, Jeeves will try to make a difference and in a meaningful way.

He hopes that others will join him in their own ways.

Jeeves also enjoys November for another reason.

He looks forward to Election Day.

Jeeves is thankful that we live in a democracy.

This year, he won't be waiting to hear election results.

Next year will be different.

Jeeves will be waiting to hear the results of our presidential, federal, state, county and city elections.

He's already started to wonder about Lincoln's election.

Next year, Lincoln will elect three city councilmen.

Jeeves is thankful that Lincoln does not have to contend with a recall election before next November.

While he respects the right to petition for change, Jeeves is happy that the recall is over.

And he's happiest for a reason that some might not expect.

Sure, the cost of a recall troubled him.

And the divisiveness troubled him more.

But the prospect of a leadership void troubled him most.

The recall proponents told us who they didn't want but they didn't tell us who they did want.

Between now and next November's election, Jeeves hopes that candidates emerge for all open offices.

Jeeves wonders what the recall proponents want in a candidate for Lincoln's City Council.

And he also wonders what other voters want in a leader.

Do they want someone presidential like?

If so, do they want a Ronald Reagan type or a Jimmy Carter type of leader?

Do they want someone business like?

If so, do they want a Donald Trump type or a Warren Buffett type of leader?

Do they want someone activist like?

If so, do they want an Ann Coulter type or a Jane Fonda type of leader?

Do they want a celebrity?

If so, do they want an Arnold Schwarzenegger type or George Clooney type of leader?

Jeeves is a big fan of Clooney.

He might be tempted to vote for him.

But Jeeves knows that just because George Clooney plays the part of a candidate during his current movie release, *Ides of March,* doesn't mean that he qualifies as a candidate for Lincoln's City Council.

Before casting a vote, Jeeves would want to know more about Clooney's qualifications.

First, Jeeves would try to find out how much he knows about Lincoln.

Then, Jeeves would try to find out what experience he has gained by serving on Lincoln's committees and boards.

And Jeeves would try to find out about his performance.

Did he attend regularly and participate fully?

Or did he show up just for screen credits?

Jeeves would also try to find out if he earned his top billing positions.

Or is he really a bit player with a pretty face and family connections?

To what extent to has he given back or made a difference?

Jeeves would try to get him to identify what he believes are Lincoln's biggest issues.

Does he have a plan to deal with them?

Or will he offer more of the same?

Jeeves would ask him to explain what he would do during an emergency such as a tanker fire.

Would he be stay in town and perform like former New York Mayor Rudy Giuliani who was heroic during 9/11?

Or would he leave town?

Jeeves would want to know if he could speak for himself.

Or would he have to rely on scripts written by others?

Jeeves would want to know if he could think for himself.

Or would his performance depend on the direction of others?

Jeeves would want to know if he finds it important to do what's right for Lincoln?

Or if he finds it more important to do what's politically expedient?

There's no doubt that Clooney would be good to look at during City Council meetings.

But without answers to his many questions, Jeeves doesn't know if he would be good for Lincoln.

While they may not be quite as good to look at, Jeeves does know that there are three men who have been good for Lincoln.

Thanks to them, Lincoln was not faced with a leadership void.

Jeeves has been tough on all three.

Yet, they have withstood slings and arrows from him and from others.

Despite criticisms and threat of recall, Councilman Tom Cosgrove, Mayor Paul Joiner and Mayor Pro Tem Spencer Short remain steadfast.

This year, Jeeves gives thanks that none were recalled.

And, he gives thanks that all three continue to serve in their own meaningful ways.

Jeeves enjoys November.

It's time to give thanks.

🐾 NEW TRICKS...

Jeeves loves words.

He admires anyone who uses words effectively.

So he especially admires writers.

Some write poems.

Some write plays.

Some write books.

Some write essays.

Some write speeches.

During this election season, Jeeves heard many speeches.

He learned that some speech writers are better than others.

Lincoln is blessed to have many writers.

Jeeves believes that they are wonderful.

The writers he knows don't write speeches.

Lincoln resident Fran Neves writes poems.

Her poem, "Politicians," was featured in the Nov. 1 *Lincoln News Messenger* (Page A5, "Election time prompts poem on politicians").

Neves will read her poems during the Poets Club of Lincoln meeting this Sunday (3 p.m., Willow Room, Twelve Bridges Library).

Lincoln resident Jeri Chase Ferris writes books (jerichaseferris.com).

Ferris' most recent book is called *Noah Webster And His Words*.

It was released Oct. 23.

This book is Ferris' 11th biography and it's receiving rave reviews.

Noah Webster knew all about words.

Webster's dictionary bears his name.

Lincoln resident Dick Huser also writes books.

He wrote *Confessions of a Sinister Minister* and *My Anxiety Is Better Than Your Anxiety*.

Jeeves enjoys hearing from Neves, Ferris and Huser.

He's flattered that these wonderful writers take time to write to him.

Jeeves also admires writers who make others' words more effective.

Lincoln resident Carol Feineman is editor of *Lincoln News Messenger*.

Not only is she a great writer but she helps Jeeves and others organize the words that appear in *Lincoln News Messenger*.

Lincoln resident Sue Clark writes memoirs.

She's also a poet, a literary agent and a ghostwriter.

Jeeves was surprised to discover that, as a ghostwriter, Clark doesn't write about ghosts.

Instead, she writes on behalf of others.

One day, he hopes to rise to the high standards set by Lincoln's great writers.

Jeeves can only dream of writing like writers who are known throughout the world such as William Shakespeare.

In *Hamlet* (Act II, Scene II), Shakespeare wrote "brevity is the soul of wit."

At the other end of the spectrum, Jeeves also dreams of writing like Dorothy Parker.

Jeeves enjoys her witticisms.

For *Vogue* (1916), she wrote, "Brevity is the soul of lingerie.

Jeeves especially likes Parker's, "You can't teach an old dogma new tricks."

Parker also wrote, "This is not a novel to be tossed aside lightly. It should be thrown with great force."

Jeeves could not imagine tossing aside anything by Shakespeare or Parker.

Nor could he imagine tossing aside anything by any one of Lincoln's writers, even the ones he fails to understand.

Jeeves doesn't understand what City of Lincoln Councilman Gabriel Hydrick meant in his *Lincoln News Messenger* column "An Introduction to Mormons and their role in government (Page A8, Nov. 1).

According to our Constitution's First Amendment and our belief in separation of church and state, Jeeves wonders why Hydrick believes that Mormons, or any other religion for that matter, should have a role in our government.

But just as the First Amendment protects religious freedom, it also protects our other freedoms, including speech and the press.

So Hydrick has the right to express his point of view just as *Lincoln News Messenger* has the right to print it.

Dorothy Parker said, "I hate writing, I love having written."

Jeeves loves words.

Unlike Parker, he loves writing.

But like Parker, Jeeves loves having written.

And this little dog looks forward to learning new tricks.

🐾 MINUTE BY MINUTE...

Jeeves always watches Lincoln City Council meetings.

He enjoyed watching all of the October 28 meeting.

Due to technical difficulties, Jeeves missed hearing the first 20 minutes of the meeting.

There was no sound.

By Item 7 of the city council agenda, Jeeves could hear "Citizens Addressing Council" and the balance of the agenda.

It was an interesting meeting.

Jeeves learned a lot.

He learned about the success of October 18's Lincoln Regional Airport Open House Day.

He learned that there are advocates for medical marijuana despite a pending city ordinance to prohibit marijuana cultivation within the city limits.

He learned about a grant by Lincoln Hills Foundation that will allow Lincoln's Police Department to purchase defibrillators.

He learned about a landlord's frustration over a property that he's trying to lease at the north end of Lincoln.

He learned more about city committees due to an exchange between the City Treasurer Terrence Dorsey, Mayor Gabriel Hydrick and Councilman Paul Joiner.

And, thanks to this discussion, Jeeves heard a suggestion from another citizen who addressed city council.

This citizen's name is Dan Karleskint.

Mr. Karleskint attends most city council meetings.

During this meeting, he suggested that all committees keep minutes of their meetings.

Jeeves believes that Mr. Karleskint's suggestion is a great one.

Minutes would help eliminate any confusion about committee and staff recommendations.

Many, like Jeeves, believe that all city committees should compile a written record of their meetings.

Unfortunately, most City of Lincoln committees fail to keep minutes.

Yet, all publish their meeting agendas.

As far as Jeeves could determine, the only city committee to compile and publish minutes is Lincoln's planning commission.

Barring attendance at all city committee meetings, it's difficult to know what transpires at city committee meetings.

Over the years, Jeeves has found this frustrating.

Jeeves relies on Lincoln's city Councilman to report at the end of council meetings.

Details are often scant.

Some Councilmen are better at reporting than others.

At one time, Councilman Paul Joiner wanted to cease giving committee reports altogether.

Jeeves hopes that City of Lincoln adopts Mr. Karleskint's suggestion as soon as possible.

Meanwhile, Jeeves is grateful to Councilman Peter Gilbert who requested that the Economic Development Committee present quarterly status reports.

Although not as beneficial as minutes, they inform and provide some degree of accountability.

The second Economic Development quarterly presentation to city council took place October 28.

New Economic Development Director Shawn Tillman made his first presentation.

He shared duties with Economic Development Committee chairman Wayne Sisneroz who made his second presentation.

Jeeves believes that Mr. Tillman could have benefitted from access to the Economic Development Committee meeting minutes, if they existed.

If so, Jeeves believes that Mr. Tillman's presentation might have been more accurate and thorough.

During Mr. Tillman's remarks, he showed a series of slides about City of Lincoln's economic developments since July 2014.

He presented a slide that showed five unnamed new industrial prospects and 20 unnamed new retail prospects.

Jeeves was happy to learn about new business activity.

Additionally, Mr. Tillman remarked that he visited nine existing businesses.

As he indicated to city council, business retention is as important as business development.

One of Mr. Tillman's slides showed new businesses that will occupy space in Parkway Plaza, often called, Lowe's plaza.

According to Mr. Tillman, these new businesses include AM/PM, Baskin and Robbins, Big 5 Sporting Goods and Dollar Tree Store.

And, according to Mr. Tillman, all are due to start business in November 2014.

If Mr. Tillman had access to Economic Development Committee minutes, he might have known that Dollar Tree Store opened a year ago - November 1, 2013.

Because he's new to the city, Jeeves believes that Mr. Tillman may have confused Dollar Tree Store with another discount store.

Family Dollar Store opened in downtown Lincoln in July 2014.

Additionally, Mr. Tillman remarked about available properties for occupancy near Lincoln Regional Airport.

In particular, he addressed a city-owned property at 2000 Flightline Drive.

Mr. Tillman indicated that he looks forward to receiving feedback from those who have interest in this property, specifically prospective uses.

Jeeves was surprised to hear these comments from Mr. Tillman.

After all, Economic Development Committee persuaded city council to approve $42,000 on the OppSites program in June 2014.

This program (oppsites.com) is supposed to generate prospective uses for buildings and property sites so the city can market this information to investors and developers.

If Mr. Tillman had to access to any Economic Development Committee minutes, he might have known about this important and expensive development tool.

Of course, access to such minutes assumes that Economic Development Committee has something to record.

During Economic Development Committee Chairman Wayne Sisneroz's part of the presentation, he indicated that a downtown subcommittee is now going to review the Gruen and Gruen report.

This report was presented in 2010 and cost the City of Lincoln $30,000.

Jeeves is pleased that Mr. Sisneroz and his committee are finally getting around to looking at it.

Besides acting as Chair of Economic Development Committee, Mr. Sisneroz is President of Downtown Lincoln Association.

So far, all he's offered are two quarterly reports, four new economic development subcommittees and food trucks in downtown Lincoln.

Jeeves wonders what else Mr. Sisneroz has been up to over the last four years.

Without access to minutes neither Jeeves nor most anyone else really knows.

Perhaps Mr. Sisneroz could record the minutes of Economic Development Committee meetings.

And, perhaps he could indicate on the minutes "actions required" and "deadlines."

That way, we might know more about what's going on and when we can expect results.

But, here's what we do know about Economic Development Committee.

City of Lincoln pays Mr. Tillman more than $90,000 per year.

His salary, combined with thousands of dollars spent on programs, consultants' reports and consultants, represents a big investment.

So, Jeeves is looking for a return on this city's investment by the end of the next quarter.

He can wait another three months.

But, he can't wait another four years and neither should city council.

Dan Karleskint's suggestion about committee meeting minutes is a great one.

And, it didn't cost the city anything.

Jeeves believes that minutes for city committees are overdue.

He can hardly wait for the city to publish the minutes of all committee meetings.

He expects to learn a lot just like he does when he watches city council meetings.

And, Jeeves won't need any sound when he reads them.

🐾 LEST WE FORGET...

Lest we forget.

Nov. 11 is a special day.

Nov. 11 is Veterans Day.

Veterans Day is also known as Armistice Day and Remembrance Day.

Armistice Day commemorates the 1918 Armistice between the Allies of World War I and Germany.

Lest we forget.

At the 11th hour on the 11th day of the 11th month, many throughout the world will stop whatever they're doing to pay tribute to more than 60 million people who died in that war and the wars that followed.

Lincoln is no exception.

On Friday, in front of Veterans Memorial Hall, 541 Fifth St., a ceremony will honor Lincoln's veterans, starting at 11:11 a.m.

Lest we forget.

Jeeves will also pay tribute.

Like others, he will stop whatever he's doing to remember more than 840,000 casualties from the Battle at Passchendaele.

Many, who were not killed in battle, drowned in 10-plus feet of mud.

Some are just now rising to the surface.

Like others, Jeeves will remember the 10,000 casualties of chlorine gas from the second battle at Ypres.

Like others, he will remember more than 1,200,000 casualties from the Battle of the Somme.

Machine gunner George Coppard wrote: "Hundreds of dead were strung out like wreckage washed up to a high water-mark. Quite as many died on the enemy wire as on the ground, like fish caught in the net. They hung there in grotesque postures. Some looked as if they were praying; they had died on their knees and the wire had prevented their fall. Machine gun fire had done its terrible work."

Lest we forget.

Like others, Jeeves will remember more than 37 million casualties of World War 1 from all battles during the four years between 1914 and 1918.

And, like others, Jeeves will remember to honor more than 8.5 million of those who sacrificed their lives in what, ironically, we refer to as the "war to end all wars."

Lest we forget.

Then, like others, he will remember more than 5,930,000 casualties from World War II, of which 1,076,245 were American wounded.

And, like others, Jeeves will remember that more than 405,000 Americans made the ultimate sacrifice during this war.

Lest we forget.

Like others, Jeeves will remember more than 392,000 casualties from the Korean War of which Americans accounted for more than 133,000 wounded.

He will also remember that 36,516 Americans lost their lives.

Lest we forget.

Like others, Jeeves will remember more than 211,000 American wounded from the Viet Nam War and the 58,272 Americans killed in action.

Lest we forget.

Like others, Jeeves will remember 1,231 American wounded from the first Gulf War and the 258 Americans who died.

Lest we forget.

Like others, Jeeves will remember more than 46,957 coalition casualties from the War on Terror and 7,578 coalition troops who have lost their lives, as of Nov. 6, 2011.

Lest we forget.

Like others, Jeeves will take time out to give thanks for all the extraordinary men and women who have served and continue to serve in military forces in this country and in allied countries throughout the world.

Nov. 11 is a special day.

Nov. 11 is Veterans Day.

Lest we forget.

🐾 DOGGED...

Jeeves enjoys this time of year.

He especially likes to see the leaves change color.

Jeeves also likes cooler weather.

Lower temperatures mean that Jeeves can wear his trench coat.

When he wears his trench coat, Jeeves believes that he looks like newspaperman Clark Kent.

He was a reporter for *The Daily Planet*.

But this was just a disguise for Superman.

Jeeves wishes he could be a reporter like Clark Kent and a crime fighter like Superman.

So he asked the Downtown Dogs for advice.

The dogs reminded Jeeves that Clark Kent was a reporter.

"Jeeves," they said "You're a columnist, not a reporter. You're no Superman, either. And, Superman wore a cape, not a trench coat. You're not faster than a speeding bullet. You're not more powerful than a locomotive. You can't leap tall buildings in a single bound. You can't fly. And you don't have superhuman strength."

Alas, Jeeves discovered that donning a trench coat wouldn't make him Clark Kent much less Superman.

The dogs told Jeeves that he should forget about being a reporter and a crime fighter.

"It's not a role for dogs," they said.

Jeeves was undeterred.

"What about Bulldog Drummond?" he asked. "If a bulldog can be a crime fighter, why can't a Yorkshire terrier be one too?"

The dogs reminded Jeeves that Bulldog Drummond was not a dog.

Instead, it was anickname of a fictional character called Caption Hugh "Bulldog" Drummond that was created by Herman Cyril McNeile under his pseudonym "Sapper."

"What about *The Hound of the Baskervilles*?" Jeeves asked.

The dogs reminded Jeeves that the hound was not the crime fighter.

Instead, it was Sherlock Holmes who discovered the questionable role of the hound in this deadly mystery.

"Give it up, Jeeves!" they said. "It's all fiction."

But Jeeves was not going to settle for being just a little dog in a beige coat.

Despite the Downtown Dogs' admonishments, he searched and searched for a crime-fighting dog.

And his dogged determination paid off.

Jeeves found a canine crime fighter.

His name is Spy.

And like Jeeves, Spy is a Yorkshire terrier.

Spy is also a columnist.

He writes for a new magazine, *Just the Facts*.

Spy's column is called "Spy's Corner."

In his recent column, Spy offers tips for babysitting safety.

But, best of all, he works with real life private investigator Frank Roman, who has been tracking down criminals for more than 35 years.

Spy also makes personal appearances at special events along with Roman.

He's famous in crime-fighting circles.

Jeeves can hardly wait to tell the Downtown Dogs about meeting Spy.

There's nothing fictional about him

Jeeves will be sure to wear his trench coat.

And maybe he'll start looking for a cape.

🐾 NO BONES ABOUT IT...

Jeeves enjoys downtown Lincoln.

He likes spending time with the Downtown Dogs around the fountain in Beermann Plaza.

After they chew on a few bones, the dogs like to people watch.

From their vantage point, they can see F Street and they can see the alleyway that runs between Fifth and Sixth Streets.

They see many people come and go.

Some hurry.

Some dawdle.

Some stop to shop.

Some stop to dine.

Last week, they observed a group of men who stopped to eat their lunch together at Kim's Country Kitchen.

It's not the first time the Downtown Dogs have seen them meet to eat.

These men are easily identifiable due to the number times they eat at the same place, in the same backroom and at the same table.

These men serve on City of Lincoln's Economic Development Committee.

The dogs are happy to see them support a downtown business.

But, the dogs wonder if these men are cognizant of California's Brown Act when they sit down together for lunch.

The Brown Act governs meetings of public bodies, like City Council and city committees.

Under the Brown Act, a public meeting requires notice and an agenda in accordance with certain time schedules.

Anyone who watches Lincoln City Council meetings has learned that no more than two City Councilmen can meet, other than during a City Council meeting, to discuss issues.

Simply stated, if a majority of City Council meets, it's considered a public meeting.

Lincoln City Council has five members.

Therefore, three Councilmen represent a majority of City Council.

Any meeting of three or more Councilmen requires public notice and agenda regardless of how, when, why and where they meet.

This also means that it's unlikely the dogs will see more than two City Councilmen chew on a few bones around the fountain in Beermann Plaza without public notice and an agenda.

During the October 28th City Council meeting, Councilman Paul Joiner expressed his concerns over Brown Act issues that involve more than two city Councilmen at City committee meetings.

Two Councilmen are assigned to each City committee.

Councilman Stan Nader regularly attends committee meetings including those to which he is not assigned.

The Downtown Dogs applaud him for taking extra time to learn about city issues at the committee level despite any concerns over the Brown Act.

The dogs know that Councilman Nader goes out of his way to attend extra committee meetings as an observer only.

In his capacity, as an observer, Councilman Nader is careful to be expressionless.

Councilman Nader knows that any verbal or facial expression could be interpreted as opinion.

As such, either could mean a violation of the Brown Act.

The dogs recognize that it must be difficult for Councilman Nader, or any Councilman, to sit on the sidelines especially during discussion of serious and contentious issues.

But, as difficult as it may be, Councilman Nader has shown that he understands the provisions of the Brown Act and adheres to them.

The Downtown Dogs wonder if members of City committees recognize that they have the same obligations under the Brown Act as our City Councilmen.

For City of Lincoln committees, a majority may depend on the size of the committee or the number that the committee sets as a quorum.

City of Lincoln committees vary in size.

Based on information that the dogs found through the city's website, Finance Committee appears to have one member plus two City Councilmen for a total of three.

Based on information from the city's website, Economic Development Committee appears to have seven members plus two city Councilmen and one city staff for a total of ten.

Without knowing how many members comprise each committee or constitute quorum, it's difficult for the dogs to know what forms a majority for either of these committees.

For Finance Committee, a majority could be two members or it could be one.

For Economic Development Committee a majority could be six members or it could be four.

The dogs suspect that the larger number applies otherwise all actions of one Finance Committee member would require public notice and agenda.

But, the dogs' suspicions don't count.

What does count are the laws that govern public meetings according to the Brown Act.

For this reason, members of all city committees should check the laws and their status before they sit down together for lunch.

Otherwise, they may find that they wind up with more bones than they can chew.

They may find that they have violated the Brown Act.

🐾 GIMME SHELTER...

Jeeves looks forward to Thursday.

He enjoys Thanksgiving.

He especially likes Thanksgiving dinner.

Before dinner, it's customary for Jeeves' family to say grace and give thanks.

Jeeves has a lot to be thankful for this year.

And, he will take time to express his thanks before he digs into his turkey and gravy.

Jeeves is thankful for his family.

They ensure that he's well nourished by feeding him.

They ensure that he's healthy by keeping him vaccinated against illnesses.

They ensure that he's safe by keeping him on a leash.

They ensure that he's recoverable by registering his microchip.

They ensure that he's legal by licensing him with Placer County.

And, they ensure that he's well-rested by providing a bed.

Jeeves is grateful that his family cares.

He knows that there are many dogs and cats that are not as fortunate.

Jeeves sees animals roam the streets.

They have no one who cares for them or about them.

Some animals are rescued from a life on the streets.

They are placed in animal shelters.

They must wait until their owners claim them or someone adopts them.

Jeeves has visited Placer SPCA shelter.

It's a clean and safe place.

But, it's not as nice as his home.

Jeeves discovered approximately 3.9 million dogs and 3.4 million cats enter shelters every year.

ASPCA (www.aspca.org) reports that approximately 542,000 dogs and 100,000 cats are returned to their owners.

And, approximately 1.4 million dogs and 1.3 million cats are adopted each year.

Jeeves doesn't like to think about what happens to the remaining 1.2 million dogs and 1.4 million cats.

ASPCA estimates that there are 13,600 shelters across the United States.

But, there's no national organization to monitor these shelters or tabulate statistics.

As a result, there may be many more stray dogs and cats.

Jeeves is grateful for two nearby animal shelters.

In Auburn, Placer County provides a shelter which is located at 11251 B Avenue.

In Roseville, Placer SPCA provides a shelter at 150 Corporation Yard Road.

Jeeves is also grateful for the many pet rescue organizations.

In Lincoln, FieldHaven Feline Rescue is located 2754 Ironwood Lane.

Jeeves knows that these shelters and rescue organizations work hard to place animals in good homes.

He also knows that supply is greater than demand.

And, he also knows that costs to maintain shelters and rescue are high.

Through Placer SPCA, Jeeves learned that a donation of $15 can help feed and vaccinate a dog or cat.

He learned that a donation of $25 can help spay or neuter a pet.

And, he learned that $50 can help an animal receive emergency surgery.

Before Jeeves digs into his dinner on Thursday, he will give thanks to all those who help pets.

He will also dig into his savings.

Jeeves will make a donation to help a less fortunate dog or cat.

🐾 ON YOUR HEELS...

Jeeves likes to sniff around the Internet.

He likes to check out the pet food websites.

But, all they do is make him hungry.

Sadly, Jeeves never finds anything on these websites that nourish his body.

From time to time, Jeeves does find websites that nourish his mind.

Last week, Jeeves discovered a website about Lincoln Center.

Jeeves was ecstatic.

Finally, he found a website that extolls downtown Lincoln's attributes.

Alas, Jeeves was mistaken.

The website was not referring to the center of Lincoln, CA.

Instead, the website was referring to a center in New York, NY.

Jeeves learned that New York's Lincoln Center is for the performing arts.

It covers over 16 acres.

And, Lincoln Center for the Performing Arts includes over 30 indoor and outdoor performance facilities such as Avery Fisher Hall, Metropolitan Opera House and Alice Tully Hall.

And, Lincoln Center is home to New York City Ballet, Juilliard School, New York Philharmonic and eight other resident arts organizations.

Lincoln Center grew out of a 1950's urban renewal project led by John D. Rockefeller III and other civic leaders.

A "blighted area" was transformed into a one of the world's leading cultural centers.

Jeeves wondered if downtown Lincoln could have a Lincoln Center too.

After all, downtown Lincoln already has seven facilities.

Downtown Lincoln is home to the Carnegie Library, Civic Center, Lincoln Area Archives Museum, Art League of Lincoln and McBean Park Pavilion.

Jeeves believes that they offer a great base for indoor arts.

Downtown Lincoln also has Beermann Plaza and McBean Park

Jeeves believes that they offer a complementary base for outdoor arts.

More importantly, downtown Lincoln is not a "blighted area" in need of urban renewal.

But, most everyone agrees that it's an area that's in need of revitalization.

Jeeves believes that downtown Lincoln could be transformed into a cultural center for our city.

Over time, Jeeves believes the downtown Lincoln could also become a leading cultural center for Placer County and beyond.

Jeeves called a meeting of the Downtown Dogs to discuss the idea of a Lincoln's Center.

They met around the fountain in Beermann Plaza.

Jeeves told them about New York's Lincoln Center for the Performing Arts.

The dogs reviewed all seven existing facilities in Downtown Lincoln.

They agreed that these facilities represent a solid base.

But, they also agreed that not all facilities are suitable for staging large performance productions like operas and symphonies.

"It's all a matter of scale," said Downtown Dog Luna.

"Why limit ourselves to performing arts?" asked Simon. "we should include all the arts."

The Downtown Dogs agreed with Simon.

Lincoln's downtown buildings and plaza represent opportunities for staging different types of visual, literary and performance arts - some small and some larger.

"How do we pay for our Lincoln's Center? asked Mabel.

"Does John D. Rockefeller live in Lincoln?"

The dogs agreed that Mabel's questions needed answers.

"If Rockefeller does live in Lincoln, you can bet his house is in Sun City Lincoln Hills," said Mabel.

"And, if it is, we're doomed."

"What makes you say we're doomed?" asked the dogs.

"Sun City Lincoln Hills already has its own facilities," said Mabel.

"Why would they support downtown facilities?"

The Downtown Dogs challenged Mabel.

They reminded her that Sun City has always been a big supporter of Lincoln activities no matter where they occur in the city.

And, they asked her, why any one person or any one area of the city should be expected to be a bigger contributor than any other person or area of the city?

Just the same, the Downtown Dogs wondered about paying for Lincoln's Center.

Then, Luna reminded them that the buildings, the plaza and the park already exist.

"I don't believe that the idea of Lincoln's Center depends on money as much as it depends on having a vision and developing a plan," stated Luna.

"For now," Luna said "I believe that we need a group of visionaries to develop a plan."

"But, we already have Downtown Lincoln Association," declared Jeeves.

The dogs howled in unison.

They reminded Jeeves that, after more than three years, Downtown Lincoln Association has only been able to come up with a monthly food truck event as its best idea for downtown's revitalization.

That event may nourish the body but does nothing for the mind.

"No," said Luna "I believe that we need our city council to appoint an Arts Commission, like Planning Commission, to come up with a strategic plan that takes into account all the arts and this city's venues."

The dogs agreed with Luna.

But, how they would go about getting city council to take action?

Simon reminded the dogs that this is an election year.

"If we start nipping at candidates' heels now," Simon said "we can start to make a difference."

Luna reminded the dogs that it took many years for Lincoln Center for the Performing Arts to become what it is today.

"So, we have to go beyond election candidates," emphasized Luna.

"We have to nip at the heels of city council and the entire electorate, especially the well-heeled who have influence."

Jeeves left the meeting encouraged by his discussion with the Downtown Dogs.

He believes that Lincoln will have a Lincoln's Center someday.

And, he believes that such a center will not only revitalize but transform Lincoln's downtown into a place that can nourish the body and the mind.

For now, Jeeves is out looking for heels to nip.

🐾 VISIONARY...

Jeeves looks forward to the day when the Lincoln bypass is complete.

He knows that downtown Lincoln will be different as a result.

As a minimum, there will be less traffic and it should be safer to cross G Street.

Representatives of downtown businesses have started meeting with the city's economic development department to develop plans that will make our city an even more attractive destination.

Jeeves hopes that our business leaders will take time and come up with a new vision to reshape downtown Lincoln.

He has observed, first hand, the transforming power of one person with a vision.

This summer, Jeeves was able to take a sneak peak at Beermann Plaza when it was turned into a magical place that literally took his breath away.

Jeeves loves Beermann Plaza.

Both he and the Downtown Dogs did not think it could look better.

It can.

One Saturday, Diana Burke of Simple Pleasures Catering turned Beermann Plaza into the perfect setting for an evening wedding.

Her vision for this exciting and joyous ceremony rivaled anything that could come from any movie studio.

Neither words nor photos can do justice to Diana's creation.

You had to see it to believe it.

It was truly memorable.

One person - one vision made a difference to downtown.

Not too long after, Jeeves learned that Diana was challenged, once again, to come up with a totally different vision for Beermann Plaza.

Sadly, Bruce Stone, the father of the bride, died suddenly.

Diana was asked to transform the plaza into a fitting site for his memorial service.

She succeeded using more of her creative talents for this somber and sorrowful occasion.

Our business leaders now have a great opportunity to transform all of downtown.

They can make it a destination that attracts from visitors from Lincoln and beyond.

Their success will depend on the scope their imaginations.

Jeeves hopes that they, like Diana, dream big!

🐾 NEWS VERSUS VIEWS...

Now that the days are cooler, Jeeves spends more time outdoors with the Downtown Dogs.

They meet more often in Beermann Plaza.

Last week, the dogs asked Jeeves why he failed to write-up their news tip.

Jeeves reminded the Downtown Dogs that he is not a reporter.

When he receives a news tip, Jeeves gives it to Editor Carol Feineman.

She decides what is newsworthy and who will write the story.

Early in his brief writing career, Jeeves submitted a story that contained news.

That story did not make it into print nor was it posted on-line.

The editor reminded Jeeves that he's a commentator not a reporter.

Jeeves can comment only on stories that appear in *Lincoln News Messenger* or in the public domain.

However, the Downtown Dogs reminded Jeeves that Kathy Dorsey writes about Lincoln events.

They wanted to know why Kathy can report but Jeeves can't.

The dogs wondered if the Editor has something against dogs.

"No," Jeeves told them.

He explained that Kathy does not report news.

Instead, she usually promotes events that have yet to occur.

As a result, these events are not yet news.

But, the Downtown Dogs reminded Jeeves that Kathy also writes about events that have occurred.

Jeeves explained to the dogs that these events are not considered news.

"Not news!" they yelped.

"Won't the Knights of Columbus be surprised to find out that this weekend's Oktoberfest event is not news?"

As far as the dogs are concerned, all Lincoln events are news especially their meetings around the fountain.

Jeeves used to think the same way.

He's learned that the "news" is different.

And, the business of news can be difficult to understand.

Jeeves knows that he still has much to learn.

So far, he's determined that "news" is about events that happen out of the ordinary.

News is about extraordinary events rather than routine ones.

But, the Downtown Dogs reminded Jeeves that Knights of Columbus' Oktoberfest happens once-a-year.

Their event is anything but routine.

The dogs are correct but they're not right.

Jeeves explained that it is expected that Knights of Columbus will hold fund raising events.

In October, it is equally expected that a non profit organization will hold an Oktoberfest just as it is expected another group will hold a crab feed.

To the organizers of such events who volunteer tremendous amounts of time and energy, Jeeves recognizes that there is nothing routine about them.

But, from a news reporting standpoint, these events are expected.

As such, they're not news.

If German Chancellor Angela Merkel showed up for the Oktoberfest, it would be unexpected.

As such, it would be newsworthy.

The Downtown Dogs began to understand.

Neither Jeeves nor Kathy are reporters.

Jeeves is a commentator.

Kathy is a promoter and a recorder.

The dogs went on to ask Jeeves how he selects topics.

Sometimes, Jeeves relies on newspaper and televison news reports.

Other times, he relies on books or movies.

Jeeves also reads the minutes of public meetings.

For example, he reads the Fiscal Sustainability Committee minutes.

So far, Jeeves has found nothing into which he can sink his teeth.

He wonders when the committee is going to throw us a bone.

Jeeves watches City Council meetings.

He finds them a great source for commentaries.

Jeeves often has to watch them, over and over again, to ensure that his comments are correct.

His best source for columns is Downtown Lincoln.

There, he hears off-hand comments that serve as catalysts.

Jeeves finds inspiration everywhere.

Occasionally, people approach Jeeves and try to influence him with their points of view.

Some stop by to visit while others call or E-mail.

In the news business, they call this "spin."

Jeeves resents "spin" and rebuffs any attempts with his standard response.

He's always polite and he's always courteous.

Reasonable people understand and accept his position.

He wants to remain independent and objective.

When Jeeves wants spin, he chases his tail - it's more gratifying.

Next, the dogs wanted to know how long it takes Jeeves to write his commentary.

He explained that each takes about a day to develop an outline.

Then, it takes three or four days to complete a column.

Others take longer because they involve lots of research.

Some topics are complex.

So, they're difficult to distill into seven or eight hundred words.

From time to time, Jeeves discards columns.

But, he always has three or four underway.

The dogs wondered how Jeeves gets paid - by the column or by the word.

While the news business can be complicated, this part was easy for him to answer.

Jeeves volunteers his time.

He receives no compensation and has no expectation of any.

Jeeves likes to remain autonomous.

The Downtown Dogs think Jeeves is silly to write for nothing.

But, they accept and respect his choice.

Like Jeeves, they're beginning to understand the difference between news and commentary.

As the days grow shorter, Jeeves and the dogs plan to watch the leaves on downtown Lincoln trees turn from green into vivid fall colors.

They believe that it's a newsworthy event.

Alas, it's not front page news.

And, it's not breaking news either.

🐾 SIMPLY THE BEST...

Jeeves loves leftovers.

He's not picky although he has preferences.

Jeeves enjoys pizza, pasta, polenta and pork with equal enthusiasm.

Usually, he doesn't care where his leftovers are prepared.

Jeeves enjoys home made offerings as much as most restaurant ones.

But, nothing makes his tail wag more than the sight of a styrofoam or cardboard clamshell.

Jeeves knows a clamshell means that there's a surprise inside.

And, Jeeves likes surprises.

Just the same, he tries to guess what's inside the box.

Jeeves will sniff and sniff until he detects a scent.

Will it be Buonarroti's fettuccine?

Will it be Meridian's eggs benedict?

Will it be Kim's Country Kitchen's senior cheese burger?

Or, will it be his favorite?

Will it be Simple Pleasures' steak sandwich?

If it's Thursday, Jeeves has a good chance of enjoying this special treat.

Last Thursday, October 9, Simple Pleasures celebrated its 35th anniversary.

That meant extra special treats for everyone.

Jeeves was on hand to congratulate Diana Burke and her staff for their achievement.

And, theirs is a remarkable one.

Restaurants come and go.

Lincoln has lost many during the last five years.

Jeeves quit counting after 10.

But, Simple Pleasures has been a constant and a consistent purveyor of fine food from its home at 648 Fifth Street for 35 years.

Jeeves learned that until 1991, Simple Pleasures was called Sandwich Alley.

Diana and her late husband Shawn Burke changed the name to Simple Pleasures when they took over the business from Diana's mother, Doris Flocchini.

Jeeves asked Diana why she and Shawn chose the name Simple Pleasures.

Diana knelt down and she explained to Jeeves that there were two main reasons.

One reason was that their catering business had started to exceed their restaurant business.

And, catering customers were assuming that a business called Sandwich Alley could only offer cheese and meat party platters.

Of course, their catering business was offering much more just as it does today - a broad range of menus that can be customized to meet any occasion - large or small.

The other reason was their desire "to come up with an all-encompassing name that personified and reflected food that comes from the heart and gives comfort."

Jeeves believes that they succeeded.

Yet, 23 years later, many still refer to Simple Pleasures as Sandwich Alley.

That's a testament to Doris' legacy.

In Jeeves' estimation there's nothing simple about food from Simple Pleasures.

While he derives many pleasures from everything he's tasted, Jeeves finds the flavors complex.

He loves the seasoning on the steak and the spice in the pumpkin spoon cake.

Simple Pleasures has many regulars who come in for their own pleasures.

Some prefer to come in every Monday for chicken and dumpling soup, taco salad or another favorite dish.

Some prefer to come in on other days of the week for their favorites like chilli, steak sandwiches, mixed berry rhubarb pie or lemon squares.

Some prefer to take out their meals rather than eat them in the restaurant.

And, some come in to celebrate birthdays, anniversaries and other special occasions.

But, Simple Pleasures offers more than good food.

All customers are made to feel special.

That's also why they keep coming back year after year.

Like any business, Simple Pleasures depends on the support of its regular customers.

But, there's nothing regular about a restaurant that can claim 35 years of doing business in Lincoln.

As far as Jeeves is concerned, Simple Pleasures is simply the best.

🐾 THE NEXT FOUR YEARS...

Jeeves likes to plan for the future.

City of Lincoln is no different.

The city has a plan for its future.

It's called *General Plan 2050*.

It was developed to shape our city's future.

In March 25, 2008, the city council adopted it.

General Plan 2050 is available to read on the city's website.

According to the city's website, "city actions, such as those relating to land use allocations, annexations, zoning, subdivision and design review, redevelopment, and capital improvements must be consistent with the General Plan."

Jeeves has read the *General Plan 2050*.

He believes that it's a good plan.

Others think so too.

It won an award from the American Planning Association.

This Association represents 35,000 members from more than 100 countries and is devoted to "making great communities happen."

Jeeves wanted to know what the incumbent and new candidates for city council have to offer to the city in relation to the plan.

So, Jeeves was happy to hear that three public forums were scheduled for candidates to present themselves and their ideas.

Jeeves watched every forum.

Although Jeeves found time to watch, not all candidates found time to attend.

Councilman Peter Gilbert failed to attend one of three forums.

Candidate Brandy Waters failed to attend two of three forums.

Their absences disappointed Jeeves and left him to wonder about their level of commitment.

And, their absences made it difficult for Jeeves to discern their positions specifically with respect to our General Plan.

Incumbent candidates and Councilmen Paul Joiner and Councilman Spencer Short attended all forums.

And, candidates Holly Woods Andreatta and Dan Karleskint attended all forums.

Their attendance pleased Jeeves and left no room for him to wonder about their level of commitment.

And, their attendance at these forums made it easier for Jeeves to discern their positions, especially with respect to our general plan.

Based on what he heard during the three forums, Jeeves has come away shaking his head.

He was surprised to discover that just one candidate referenced the city's General Plan during the forums.

That candidate is an incumbent, Councilman Spencer Short.

Jeeves was surprised that none of the other candidates referenced *General Plan 2050*.

But, based on what he heard during the Downtown Lincoln Association forum he shouldn't have been surprised.

During that forum, no candidate mentioned the Gruen + Gruen *Marketing Analysis and Strategic Action Plan for Downtown Lincoln* either.

Like *General Plan 2050*, it's a good plan too.

Although it didn't win any awards, it was developed after many hours of consultation with downtown Lincoln business owners and stakeholders.

It also cost the city $30,000.

Jeeves believes that the downtown plan and the general plan are this city's two most important documents.

Yet, both plans get short shrift from all candidates except incumbent Councilman Short.

Jeeves wonders if the other candidates have bothered to read either plan.

Jeeves listened carefully during all the forums.

He heard candidates Andreatta and Karleskint reference another plan.

They addressed issues in the Fiscal Sustainability Plan.

That plan was presented to city council five years ago.

Jeeves wondered why would they want to align themselves with a plan that was dead on arrival?

While the Fiscal Sustainability Plan committee was chewing up dollars and resources, city staff and city council came up with the solutions to our fiscal crisis on their own.

Karleskint served on the Fiscal Sustainability Committee.

As a result, Jeeves believes that he should know better than to reference it now.

Andreatta did not serve on that committee.

Nonetheless, Jeeves believes that she should have done her homework.

Then, she would have known, as Councilman Short reminded the audience, that city council found the idea of subcontracting police, fire and garbage services neither practical nor cost-effective.

Jeeves does support Andreatta's comments on the importance of transparency in government.

Jeeves also recognizes the extensive experience Karleskint has gained while serving on other city committees such as planning commission.

During the Downtown Lincoln Association forum, incumbent candidate Councilman Joiner shared his idea for downtown.

He wants Lincoln's downtown to look like Bend, Oregon which, if Jeeves recorded his comments correctly, is distinguished by alleyway art.

During all forums, Joiner spoke about his property development and graphic arts experience.

Based on this experience plus eight years on city council, Jeeves believes that Joiner should be able to offer Lincoln more than a street scape from another city in another state.

Jeeves is sure that Lincoln has as many artists per capita than Bend or any other city of its size.

Why doesn't Councilman Joiner look toward them for direction plus all this city's other resources?

During the Sun City Lincoln Hills forum, incumbent candidate and Councilman Peter Gilbert made Jeeves and other audience members gasp.

Gilbert explained that he wants to represent "my neighbors."

He declared this in the context of helping his Sun City neighbors in the same way he helped them fight against golf course solar panels in Lincoln Hills.

Jeeves wondered if Councilman Gilbert was simply pandering to the crowd or if he really believes that he serves on city council to represent his neighbors in Sun City only?

If Gilbert was pandering, he was offensive.

Sun City residents, like Jeeves, deserve better.

But, if Gilbert believes that he represents Sun City to the exclusion the city's other neighborhoods, he is unworthy to serve again as a city Councilman.

Instead, he should run for the board of the Sun City Lincoln Hills Association where he can serve his neighbors exclusively.

Lincoln belongs in the hands of Councilmen who are committed to representing all residents no matter where they live within the city limits.

Unfortunately, Jeeves didn't read or hear enough from Brandy Waters to know what to make of her.

Jeeves knows that incumbents tend to have the advantage in elections.

Jeeves believes that Councilman Spencer Short has earned the incumbent advantage and the right serve again.

He believes that Councilman Paul Joiner and Councilman Peter Gilbert have not earned the incumbent advantage nor the right to serve again.

Yet, because they are incumbents, Jeeves knows that he may have to look at Gilbert and Joiner during city council meetings for another four years.

Hopefully, that won't happen.

In addition to Spencer Short, Jeeves hopes to look at two new city Councilmen, Holly Woods Andreatta and Dan Karleskint over the next four years.

Jeeves knows that not all voters will share his views.

He understands.

Jeeves respects different and opposing points of views.

His hope is that voters will also take a hard long look at all city council candidates to form their own views before they complete their ballots.

Unfortunately, voters will not have the benefit of additional forums to hear from the candidates.

So, Jeeves encourages voters to read the September 29, 2016 and October 6, 2016 editions of the *Lincoln News Messenger*.

They are available online and include statements from all candidates regarding many issues, including the general plan.

Jeeves likes to plan for the future.

Yet, he knows that the results of our city's election, like all elections, are unpredictable.

The best people may lose.

That's why Jeeves is grateful that our city has an award-winning plan.

🐾 COMIC RELIEF...

Jeeves likes comedians.

They make him laugh.

Jeeves likes to laugh.

One of his favorite comedians was Joan Rivers.

Sadly, she died recently.

Jeeves will miss her brash humor.

But, he'll treasure the photo of her that she took time to autograph and send.

Jeeves also enjoys other comedians who appear on television.

He likes the watching the comedians on Blue Collar Comedy Tour.

Jeeves enjoys Jeff Foxworthy.

So much so that Jeeves discovered that he might be a "redneck."

Jeeves also enjoys Larry the Cable Guy and Bill Engvall.

But, his favorite Blue Collar comedian is Ron White.

As part of his comedic act, Ron White regularly sips scotch.

And, he calls himself "Tater Salad" for which he has become famous.

Jeeves calls him "funny" although he knows that Ron White may not be everyone's cup of whiskey.

And, his comedy may not be suitable for children or puppies.

In his act, Ron White often makes jokes about his dog named "Sluggo."

That's another reason why Jeeves enjoys him so much.

On his website, tatersalad.com, Sluggo appears with a cigar in his mouth.

But, Ron White may be best known for his expression "You can't fix stupid."

His expression is so famous that it appears on videos, compact discs and t-shirts.

At first, Jeeves wasn't sure what Ron White meant when he said "You can't fix stupid."

After all, Jeeves has been "fixed."

But, after hearing more of Ron White's act, Jeeves discovered that his medical procedure had nothing to do with stupidity or any other character trait.

No, Ron White means something else when he says "You can't fix stupid."

Jeeves discovered that Ron White means that there are some people who will always fail to understand certain issues no matter how much you try to educate them.

What is obvious to the rest of us is lost on them.

Others might say, "They just don't get it" instead of "You can't fix stupid."

Young people might say "Duh!"

Jeeves has met people who don't get it.

He's even met some dogs who don't get it despite having been "fixed."

Jeeves just shakes his head.

He shook his head last week.

Once again, Downtown Lincoln Association proved that it doesn't get it.

Jeeves has written before about the food trucks that Downtown Lincoln Association brings to downtown once a month.

These food trucks compete with downtown restaurants and interfere with access to other businesses.

Discouraged by Downtown Lincoln Association, 12 business owners signed and presented a letter to city council in April.

They asked for food trucks to be moved to another location.

Alas, nothing changed in six months except a change in day.

The food trucks now appear on the first Tuesday of the month rather than the first Wednesday.

Friday, October 10, Downtown Lincoln Association held a Chocolate Lover's Ball in conjunction with Lincoln Community Foundation's Chocolate Lover's Festival.

Jeeves hoped that Downtown Lincoln Association would retain the services of a downtown Lincoln restaurant or caterer to prepare the $75 per person dinner.

Sadly, it didn't.

Jeeves checked with some Lincoln restaurants and caterers.

These downtown Lincoln businesses did not even get a sniff at catering this event.

Instead, Downtown Lincoln Association retained the services of a Rocklin caterer.

The irony is not lost on Jeeves.

Although Downtown Lincoln Association purports to represent the interests of downtown businesses, Jeeves believes that it has an unusual way of showing support.

Just when the association had an opportunity to build bridges with local restaurants and businesses, it failed.

In Jeeves' estimation, this association has a miserable track record.

This association failed to open a bank account for over a year.

Yet, it collected cash from participants who never received an accounting.

This association failed to obtain nonprofit status for over three years.

During the same period, at least two members of this association went to the bank and tried to appropriate funds from the previous nonprofit group of which it wanted no part.

Of course, that's against California rules that regulate nonprofit organizations.

They claimed that they didn't know.

This association is a group of business people.

But, this association doesn't seem to know a lot about business.

The irony is not lost on Jeeves.

Jeeves should be surprised but he isn't.

From Ron White, he's learned that "You can't fix stupid."

Jeeves has been listening to the candidates who are running for Lincoln City council.

Based on all that he's heard, all candidates want to improve downtown Lincoln

Two of those candidates are incumbents.

They have served on city council for the past four years.

As such, they should know what's been going on, or what's not been going on in downtown Lincoln.

And, they've had four years to make a difference.

In Jeeves' estimation, they have made no difference to downtown Lincoln.

From Ron White, he knows that "You can't fix stupid."

But, Jeeves believes that you can change stupid.

He's not optimistic about Downtown Lincoln Association's future.

Jeeves believes that a board of trade will emerge to represent the interests of downtown Lincoln businesses.

But, he's optimistic about Lincoln's future.

If we can't fix stupid, Jeeves believes that we can change it on election day.

Jeeves looks forward to November 4.

🐾 PERSPECTIVE...

Jeeves is three years old.

He's young.

Jeeves is also little.

But he's full grown.

Jeeves still has a lot to learn.

Because of his size, Jeeves is a lot closer to the ground than most everyone and everything else.

His closeness gives him a different perspective on the world.

Jeeves' perspective is relative to his size.

But he has learned that even those as close to the ground may view the world differently than him.

It depends on the way in which they look or if they look at all.

Last week, Jeeves discovered that size really doesn't matter.

He discovered that someone small and young can view the world with a larger perspective than someone twice as tall and twice as old.

Jeeves learned about Arav Karighattam.

Arav is 7-years old.

Like Jeeves, he's young.

Unlike Jeeves, he's not full grown.

And Arav has already learned a lot more than most third graders.

Arav tied Julian Ogans II for third place in the young poets' category of *Voices of Lincoln 2011 Poetry Contest* with his entry called "The World."

This is just one of Arav's 200 poems!

During this seventh annual event, a capacity crowd was on-hand to hear Arav and other poets read their award-winning entries.

Contest Chair Alan Lowe opened *Voices of Lincoln* with a poem of his own called "Dream Chasers," to honor all winners.

Alan was followed by Poets Club of Lincoln President Sue Clark who welcomed everyone to the largest contest ever.

Jeeves learned that 148 poems were submitted by 75 poets.

All offered many perspectives on our world and even the "beyond."

Jeeves wonder why some people turn-up their noses at poetry.

Most people like music.

Most people like songs.

Songs are really poems set to music.

So, Jeeves wonders why most people don't like poetry?

It's all about perspective.

Jeeves believes that it takes very special talent to write poetry.

Consider 17-year old poet Matt George.

He blended cowboys and the beat of rap music in his first-place award-winning poem, "Cowboy Rap."

Or, consider Lisa Augustine.

With equal parts of humor and insight, Lisa balanced the issue of facelifts in her first place award-winning poem, "Saving Face."

Jeeves applauds all winners and hopes for a larger venue to hear next year's Voices of Lincoln.

Jeeves believes that Avram was a first place finisher.

He does not doubt the judges' decision to award him third place.

Jeeves knows that the judges have policies and procedures to follow.

Every entry is treated fairly.

It's all about perspective.

Maybe it's because Avram, like Jeeves, is young.

Maybe it's because Avram, like Jeeves, is small.

And, maybe it's because Avram, like Jeeves, enjoys reading the English romantic poet, William Wordsworth.

Jeeves especially likes Wordsworth's poem about daffodils called "I Wandered Lonely as a Cloud."

He wonders if Avram likes it too.

Jeeves would like to lose his leash and wander "lonely as a cloud."

He wishes that he could "float on high o'er vales and hills."

Like Wordsworth, Jeeves "saw a crowd, A host, of golden daffodils."

They weren't "beside the lake" but they were "beneath the trees."

He has wandered into a "bay" of green stems.

He saw what seemed like "ten thousand" daffodils "fluttering and dancing in the breeze."

Jeeves had to look up - not down - in order to see them "Tossing their heads in a sprightly dance."

They were tall and they were golden.

But none were as tall nor as golden as Avram and the other 74 poets.

It's all about perspective.

🐾 TRICK OR TREAT...

Jeeves is excited about October 31.

It's Hallowe'en.

For this day and this day only, he will abandon the scarf that his friend Molly gave him.

Jeeves will wear a costume instead.

For Hallowe'en, he plans to appear as a pumpkin.

After the sun goes down, Jeeves' costume glows in the dark.

That's when he will go out to trick or treat.

Jeeves likes the idea of being a pumpkin for a day.

His friend Cindy has a pumpkin at the front of her house.

Jeeves discovered that there are real pumpkins and there are fake pumpkins.

Cindy's pumpkin is a real one.

On Hallowe'en, Jeeves will appear as a fake pumpkin.

In his disguise, he will try to trick his friends Molly, Cindy and his other neighbors.

Jeeves discovered that pumpkins show up in many and unimaginable ways.

He found over 50 recipes that include pumpkin.

There's pumpkin soup.

There's pumpkin ravioli.

There's pumpkin waffles.

There's pumpkin granola.

There's pumpkin muffins

There's pumpkin pie.

There's pumpkin cheesecake.

There's pumpkin ice cream.

There's pumpkin coffee.

There's pumpkin dog food.

And, there's even pumpkin donut holes.

Jeeves doesn't know how pumpkin gets into donut holes.

When Jeeves buys donuts, there's nothing in the center.

The holes are always empty.

But, he does know that pumpkins seem to be everywhere else.

Jeeves wonders why pumpkins are ubiquitous at this time of year.

And, why are they part of Hallowe'en rather than some other holiday like Valentine's Day?

Why do some people call them jack-o'-lanterns instead of pumpkins.

Who is Jack?

And, why is his last name O'Lantern?

Why is there an "O'" before his last name?

Is he Irish?

Jeeves went in search of answers to his many questions.

He checked several websites including Britannica.com, Wikipedia.com and About.com.

Jeeves learned that Hallowe'en or Halloween is a contraction of "All Hallows Eve"- the evening before All Hallows' Day or All Saints Day.

Hallowe'en occurs every October 31.

It starts a three day celebration known as Allhallowtide that also includes All Saints Day and All Souls Day.

All Saints Day occurs every November 1 and is a day of prayer for saints and martyrs of the church.

And, All Souls Day every November 2 and is a day of prayer for the souls of all the dead.

Jeeves learned that during the Medieval period, bonfires were lit "to symbolize the plight of souls lost in purgatory."

Additionally, "souling" took place which "consisted of going door-to-door offering prayers for the dead in exchange for soul cakes and other treats."

Jeeves now understood more about why we go door-to-door for treats on Hallowe'en.

But, he still didn't know why Halloween includes pumpkins and jack-o'-lanterns.

He kept digging.

Jeeves discovered that jack-o'-lantern dates back to the 17th century.

Jack-o'-lantern means "man with a lantern" or "night watchman."

According to About.com, jack-o'-lantern was also a nickname for ignis fatuus (fool's fire).

This is a natural phenomenon that creates mysterious blue lights that flicker over wetlands at night.

In folklore, these lights are associated with ghosts and fairies.

During the 1800's, "jack-o'-lantern" became the popular name for "turnip lantern."

In 1887, Thomas Darlington (The Folk Speech of South Cheshire) wrote that the turnip lantern was made by "scooping out the inside of a turnip, carving the shell into a rude representation of the human face, and placing a lighted candle inside it."

Darlington also recounts that it was customary for Catholic children to carry turnip lanterns door-to-door to represent the souls of the dead while they begged for soul cakes.

Jeeves also discovered that there's a legend about how the jack-o'lantern got its name.

According to legend, jack-o'-lantern is named after a roguish Irishman, Stingy Jack.

And, according to legend (About.com), Stingy Jack "tricked the devil into promising him that he wouldn't go to hell for his many sins."

Unfortunately, when Stingy Jack died he found that he had been barred from heaven and was doomed "to wander the earth for eternity with only an ember of hellfire to light his way."

From then on, Stingy Jack was known as Jack O'Lantern.

Jeeves learned that Irish immigrants to the United States are credited with the custom of carving pumpkins.

Then, as now, pumpkins were plentiful.

And, pumpkins are harvested in October.

Now Jeeves understood why pumpkins aren't part of Valentine's Day and holidays that occur in winter, spring and summer.

Additionally, pumpkins are nutritious and versatile.

Pumpkin flowers, seeds and flesh are edible and rich in vitamins.

So, instead of turnips, immigrants carved jack-o'-lanterns out of pumpkins and a new Hallowe'en ritual was born.

Jeeves found his discoveries about Hallowe'en, trick or treat, jack-o'-lanterns and pumpkins interesting.

Yet, he was surprised how little information he could find in any one source for such a well-known holiday.

Just the same, he looks forward to dressing up for Halloween on Friday, October 31.

But, Jeeves has lost interest in disguising himself as a pumpkin.

He doesn't want to run the risk of being carved and having a lighted candle placed inside him.

Instead, Jeeves plans to disguise himself as a donut hole.

🐾 WORLD VIEW...

Everyday, Jeeves tries to learn something new.

And, everyday, he discovers how much more there is to learn.

His is an never-ending quest for knowledge.

While curiosity may have killed the cat, it's essential to this little dog's life.

Recently, he enjoyed reading parts of the Mercer *Worldwide Cost of Living Report*.

Excerpts from the report have been published worldwide.

The report shows the cost of living ranks for 214 cities.

Jeeves learned that Luanda, Angola ranks number one with the highest cost-of-living

And, Karachi, Pakistan ranks number 214 with the lowest cost-of-living.

He also learned that New York ranks number 32.

Yet New York is the city to which all other are compared.

Los Angeles ranks number 77 while San Francisco ranks number 106.

As far as Jeeves is concerned, Lincoln is better than all 214 cities combined.

Jeeves wondered why Lincoln did not make the list.

Jeeves wondered if Lincoln was asked to participate in the survey.

If not, why not?

Jeeves also worried that Lincoln's cost of living might be off the charts.

To find out answers to his questions, Jeeves contacted Mercer.

He was directed to Principal Consultant Luc Lalonde.

Luc is based in Mercer's Montreal office and specializes in information product solutions, compensation and global mobility.

Luc e-mailed responses to Jeeves' questions.

In his email, Luc explained that cost-of-living indices are used by companies to calculate compensation packages for their expatriate employees.

Companies want to ensure that their employees maintain purchasing power when transferred abroad.

Luc went on to explain that Mercer International uses a basket of goods and services to calculate rankings.

This basket is based on typical spending patterns that are representative of all expatriates.

Luc suggested a telephone discussion so that he could expand on his answers.

Jeeves was enthusiastic about the prospect of speaking with a consultant of Luc's stature.

He was curious to find out if that basket of goods and services took into account kibble for the family dog.

Luc began the telephone discussion by asking questions about Lincoln's size and location.

Jeeves explained to Luc that Lincoln is a northern California city that is about 25 miles north of Sacramento.

He went on to explain that Lincoln has population of more than 41,000.

Jeeves was proud to tell Luc that Lincoln won the coveted All America City award in 2006.

He also told him that, until recently, Lincoln was the fastest growing city in the United States.

Luc was impressed by all of this information.

However, Luc went on to explain that these attributes were not enough to make the list.

To console Jeeves, Luc reminded him that "Quebec City did not make the list, either."

After closer inspection, Jeeves realized that Roseville also did not make the list.

That made him feel better too.

Quebec City and Roseville, like many other cities, did not make the list because they do not have companies that employ large numbers of expatriates.

Luc asked Jeeves if Lincoln has expatriates.

Jeeves informed him that this city has many expatriates.

Most come from the San Francisco Bay area.

Luc explained that in order to be an expatriate there must be movement between countries.

Many believe Lincoln's expatriates may just as well be from another country.

However, Jeeves confessed that not only are they from the same country, most are from the same state.

Unfortunately, in the worldwide scheme of things, Lincoln does not yet qualify for the list.

Jeeves appreciates the amount of very valuable time that Luc devoted to answering his questions.

Luc has an important job with an important company.

Mercer is a worldwide leader in consulting.

Jeeves hopes Mercer will open a Lincoln office.

Then, maybe big companies would follow.

Maybe Luc could run it.

But that would make him an expatriate.

Jeeves would go out of his way to make him feel welcome.

While, he knows more about Lincoln and how the great city fits into the world at large, Jeeves discovered that there is still much more to learn.

Jeeves is happy for consultants, such as Luc, and companies, such as Mercer, to whom he can turn for answers to his questions.

Like other professionals to whom Jeeves regularly turns for advice, neither Luc nor Mercer charged him a fee.

Jeeves is also happy to live in Lincoln as a citizen, rather than as an expatriate.

Lincoln will always be first on his list.

Jeeves is equally grateful that his basket is full.

And, while curiosity may have killed the cat, it remains essential to this little dog's life.

🐾 DOGS' BEST FRIEND...

Jeeves and the Downtown Dogs are happy and sad.

They're happy because Al Holland successfully sold his business.

And, they're sad because they won't see their friend Al as often.

Al Holland owned Lincoln City Barber Shop at 570 Fifth Street.

He sold his shop on Friday, August 22, 2014.

Al has now retired.

During his time as a barber, Al not only made men and boys look better, he made Lincoln a better place.

Al always said that "I sleep in Wheatland, but I live in Lincoln."

Jeeves can attest to how much Al "lived" in Lincoln.

Al looked out for his business neighbors.

But, he minded his own business.

Al wanted everyone to succeed.

He was always friendly.

Between customers, Jeeves could find Al sitting on the park bench in front his shop.

While there, Al was happy to exchange views on downtown issues.

Some issues he was for and some issues he was against.

Yet, Al was always for Lincoln.

But, he was against those who seemed to come out of no where, spent no more than fifteen minutes in Downtown Lincoln and then tried to tell us how to run our businesses.

Al chose to ignore these "experts" and run his business his way.

Jeeves and the Downtown Dogs enjoyed watching Al run his business his way.

Al was an engaging professional who provided excellent service, good value and good cheer.

No one promoted Downtown Lincoln more than Al.

He did more for downtown businesses than any business group or association.

Al was a one-man chamber of commerce.

Yet, few know that Al donated his services.

He cut homeless men's hair so that they would look and feel better.

And, he cut hair for members of veterans' groups who do not have the advantages of others.

Like them, Al is a veteran.

He's Vietnam veteran.

Al shares what he has with others who are less fortunate.

He's a modest man who doesn't seek recognition.

So, he probably would prefer that no one knows of his generosity and his kindness.

But, the dogs believe that it's important for others to know of Al's many contributions to the city in which he "lived."

Al has a family.

He has three sons and one grandson.

Last week, Al was visited by his son Steve who was preparing to depart for a teaching position in Kuala Lumpur.

Jeeves remembers when Al went to South Africa to attend another son's wedding.

And, he remembers when Al became a grandfather for the first time.

These were special occasions.

Family is important to Al.

But, few know that Al showed up at this year's Lincoln High School graduation ceremony.

He went to support a young man who had no other family to watch him graduate.

Al made that night a special occasion for another man's son.

When interviewed by Wave Broadband's Gerry Lyons for a Lincoln video, Al said " Lincoln is a wonderful town - full of nice people, very historic and a good place to live."

Al is one of those nice people who became part of Lincoln's history and made this city a better place in which to live.

It's often said that a dog is a man's best friend.

As far as Jeeves and the Downtown Dogs are concerned, Al Holland is their best friend.

We miss you Al.

🐾 COMMENTERRIER...

From time to time, Jeeves has expressed opinions in this column that some readers like and some readers dislike.

He also knows that some readers don't care about his opinions at all.

While Jeeves would like his opinions to have broad-based appeal, he recognizes that not everyone shares the same point of view.

Not everyone agrees on everything.

That's no surprise to him and should be no surprise to anyone else.

But what does surprise Jeeves is the intensity to which some hold their views.

For some, there's no room for discussion, and there's no room for compromise.

These people cannot even agree to disagree.

Jeeves believes that our system of government is the best in the world.

But that doesn't mean he believes that our government always gets it right.

He likes what our federal Congress is but not all that it does.

When this happens, he might comment.

But because *Lincoln News Messenger* is a community newspaper, he probably won't.

Jeeves likes what our state legislature is but not all that it does.

When this happen, he might comment.

But because *Lincoln News Messenger* is a community newspaper, he probably won't.

The same is true of our City Council.

Jeeves likes what it is but not always what it decides is best for Lincoln.

When this happens, he might comment.

And because *Lincoln News Messenger* is a community newspaper, he probably will.

The same is also true of our chamber of commerce.

Jeeves likes what it is but not always how it represents business.

When this happens, he might comment.

And because *Lincoln News Messenger* is a community newspaper, he probably will.

Jeeves has found that when local issues trouble him, they usually trouble others as well.

How does he know?

They tell him.

Jeeves hopes that his comments will stimulate discussion.

He also hopes that varying opinions will emerge on every side of an issue.

From them, he seeks to increase his understanding and widen his viewpoint.

Jeeves tries to keep an open mind.

He regularly consults with the Downtown Dogs, the Neighborhood Dogs and the Country Dogs.

Based on those discussions, Jeeves often changes his mind.

But when all the facts have become known, he forms an opinion.

He's not afraid to express it nor should others be afraid to express theirs.

Nevertheless, that's when trouble can start.

Some people, who are used to having their own way, will often try to impose their opinions on others.

Some yell.

Some threaten.

Some bully.

Some boycott.

Some insult.

For example, last week someone even telephoned to call Jeeves "irresponsible."

And, new to the mix, some cry "vendetta."

Jeeves wasn't sure what vendetta meant.

So, he looked it up.

What he found surprised him.

Jeeves learned that vendetta means "a feud in which opposing parties murder each other."

He would never want to be a party to such an event

Jeeves would never seek to end his nor anyone else's life.

He cannot even understand the mind-set of someone who would make such an accusation.

Nor does he understand the mind-set of those who yell, threaten, bully, boycott and insult.

Although Jeeves has heard that the pen can be mightier than the sword, he has no desire to wield it in any such manner.

No, he enjoys participating in lively debates, spirited discussions, witty conversations, bright banter and plain old chit-chat.

Jeeves and the dogs enjoy attracting parties to such events.

Some may call him irresponsible.

To the paraphrase the late great lyricist Sammy Cahn, some may call him unpredictable.

And some may tell him, he's impractical.

Alas, it's rainbows Jeeves is inclined to pursue.

But what's undeniably true - he is irrepressibly interested in hearing your view.

🐾 TRAIN OF THOUGHT...

Jeeves likes trains.

The Downtown Dogs like trains too.

They like the sound of crossing gate bells that signal an oncoming train.

They like the sound of a locomotive's horn when it crosses Fifth Street,

And, most of all, they like the sound of the cars as they thump over the joints in the tracks.

Jeeves and the Downtown Dogs know that trains are an important part of Lincoln's history.

Images of trains appear on City of Lincoln's original seal which dates back to 1928 and the updated version of 2012.

Jeeves watched the August 26, 2014 Lincoln City Council meeting.

He was excited to watch a Union Pacific Railway "PowerPoint" presentation by its representative, Lisa Lawson Stark.

Jeeves learned that Union Pacific has spent over $42 billion on railway track improvements and other safety measures.

These improvements are designed to make sure that trains run safely through cities like Lincoln.

Jeeves was impressed both by the scope and depth of Ms. Lawson Starks' presentation and by the investment that Union Pacific has made with respect to safety.

Although our local newspaper reported differently, Jeeves found nothing "vague" about Ms. Lawson Stark's presentation.

Because of Federal Government regulations and Homeland Security concerns, Ms. Lawson Stark was unable to share timetables for numbers of crude oil shipments to the general public.

Jeeves was happy to hear that this information is available on a need-to-know basis.

Unlike our local newspaper, Jeeves doesn't need to know what Union Pacific carries, nor when.

And, if our local newspaper knows, many others will know too, including those who wish to do us harm.

What Jeeves does need to know is that every precaution has been taken to ensure our safety.

And Ms. Lawson Stark allayed Jeeves' fears about Union Pacific's commitment to our safety.

And, she revealed that those who do need-to-know can gain access to information that will allow them to respond in the unlikely event of a rail accident.

Many have expressed concerns about the threats that crude oil tanker cars may present to cities like Lincoln.

Jeeves understands and shares their concerns.

He remembers the tanker fire in Downtown Lincoln of three years ago.

And, he also remembers the fears that we shared until the fire was extinguished.

What surprises Jeeves is that many, including our local newspaper, who have concerns about potential threats presented by rail tanker cars, have no concerns about food truck propane tanks that roll in and out of Downtown Lincoln once a month from April to October.

The railways have spent billions on safety measures but food trucks are unregulated by this city.

In an August 28, 2014 editorial, our local newspaper expects Union Pacific to disclose its cargo and its schedules.

And, in a July 23, 2014 editorial, our local newspaper promotes the idea of food trucks despite calls for regulation and safety by business owners and residents.

A Sun City sycophant went so far as to proclaim food trucks safe in the same editorial.

This double standard troubles Jeeves.

But, over the years, both he and the Downtown Dogs have discovered that journalistic and political favoritism are more easily found in Lincoln than bones in Beermann Plaza.

The July 1, 2014 Feltonville, PA food truck propane explosion killed two and injured 11 others.

Jeeves wonders if those responsible for protecting Lincoln's residents and businesses have read the National League of Cities' 2013 report called *FOOD ON WHEELS: Mobile Vending Goes Mainstream*.

This 31-page report offers cities, like Lincoln, guidelines and best practices in order to integrate food trucks into city life.

He knows that some will argue that the risks presented by propane tanks are small compared to the risks presented by crude oil tanker cars.

But, Union Pacific has spent $42 billion to reduce the risks.

Jeeves wonders how much City of Lincoln and Downtown Lincoln Association have spent to reduce risks.

He discovered that the city gave Downtown Lincoln Association a sweetheart deal for its monthly food truck events.

When other non profit organizations want to close Fifth Street, use Beermann Plaza and set up a "bounce house," it costs at least $532.50 for each four one-half hour Class II event.

Plus, these organizations must notify property owners, provide portable toilets, hand washing stations, trash receptacles and dumpsters.

But, Downtown Lincoln Association, an association of businesses, paid a one-time fee of $175.00 for all its monthly events from April to October.

This deal represents a revenue loss of over $3,500 to City of Lincoln.

And, Downtown Lincoln Association failed to notify all property owners in advance of its first event and relies on Lincoln Area Archives Museum for toilet facilities.

Jeeves also knows that the food truck events have adversely affected 12 downtown businesses.

They signed a letter that was presented to Lincoln City Council on April 22, 2014.

In their letter, they expressed their concerns and asked for the food truck events to be moved to another Downtown Lincoln location.

And, they provided each Councilman with a copy of the National League of Cities 2013 report regarding food trucks.

Despite what our local newspaper claims, despite what Downtown Lincoln Association claims and despite what our Economic Development Committee claims, food truck events have also adversely affected downtown development.

No restauranteur is going to invest or purchase the property at 645 Fifth Street (former home Beermann's Restaurant) if food trucks are parked out front.

No sweetheart deal that includes food trucks is going to make that location more attractive to prospective investors.

National League of Cities figured it out.

Twelve downtown businesses figured it out.

The Downton Dogs figured it out.

Jeeves figured it out.

Unfortunately, neither Lincoln's City Council nor Downtown Lincoln Association have figured it out.

🐾 S'IL VOUS PLAÎT...

Jeeves likes parties.

From time to time, he receives invitations to parties.

Some invitations are for birthday parties.

Some invitations are for anniversary parties.

Some invitations are for graduation parties.

Some invitations are for wedding receptions.

And, some invitations are for other celebrations.

Most invitations refer to RSVP.

Some times RSVP is shown on a separate card.

Some times RSVP is shown next to a telephone number.

Some times RSVP is shown next to an e-mail.

And, every RSVP that Jeeves has seen refers to a certain date.

For a long time, Jeeves didn't know what RSVP meant.

In her best German accent, Jeeves great-aunt Eva told him that it stood for "remember se vedding present."

Alas, Jeeves' late great-aunt Eva was pulling his leg.

RSVP is not a German expression at all.

And, RSVP has nothing to do with wedding presents although presents may be welcome at a wedding.

As it turns out, RSVP is an abbreviation for a French expression.

RSVP stands for "répondez s'il vous plaît."

Jeeves learned that the English translation for this expression is "reply, if you please."

But, RSVP means more than this translation would have him or anyone else believe.

A "reply" to an invitation is a matter of etiquette.

"Etiquette" is also a French word.

According to www.Merriam-Webster.com, etiquette is defined as "the rules indicating the proper and polite way to behave."

Jeeves wondered about the rule of etiquette especially regarding RSVP and invitations.

So, he went in search of answers.

He read many etiquette books.

Out of the many books he read, Jeeves' found one book that he likes best.

It's called *A Book of Courtesy: The Art of Living with Yourself and Others*.

A Book of Courtesy was written by Sister Mary Mercedes, a Dominican Sister, in 1910.

Sister Mercedes wrote the book for the students at the Dominican Convent Upper School in San Rafael, California.

Later, it was distributed to students at the San Domenico School in San Anselmo, California.

Sister Mercedes reminds us that "the rules of etiquette may change, but courtesy and good manners will always be important."

She also reminds us that "Courtesy is a way of living inspired by thoughtfulness, consideration and respect for others and for yourself."

For their fiftieth class reunion, the Class of 1950 revised the book to honor the sesquicentennial of the Dominicans in California.

The revised book was published by HarperCollins in 2001.

The updated version of *A Book of Courtesy* now has guidelines for email and cell phones too.

Jeeves values his copy of this book.

His copy was given to him by friend Patricia Bleifer-Greenglass.

Jeeves believes that every home should have a copy.

Like other etiquette books, *A Book of Courtesy* directed Jeeves how to respond to an invitation.

Jeeves learned that if he receives an invitation, he should always reply.

And, he should reply promptly.

He also learned why it's important to reply.

A host needs to know how many plan to attend in order to know how much food and drink to buy.

And a prompt response is a courtesy that you extend in return to someone who was nice enough to invite you, even if it is to say that you are unable to attend.

Several weeks ago, Jeeves received an invitation to a party.

As requested, he telephoned and accepted his invitation on the same day.

A few days ago, Jeeves ran into the party's host at another function.

The host thanked Jeeves for his timely response.

The host also went on to say that more than 300 people had been invited to the upcoming party.

Alas, just 35 people have responded to date.

The host expressed disappointment over the low number of responses.

Jeeves is disappointed too.

And, he now faces a dilemma.

Jeeves wonders if he should show up early in case 300, who were invited, show up?

That way, he would make sure to get enough to eat and drink

Or, should he show up later in case 35, who took the time to respond, show up?

That way, he would make sure to get even more enough to eat and drink - maybe leftovers.

Then, he remembered what he read in *A Book of Courtesy*.

Jeeves will show up on time.

He knows that punctuality is a courtesy too.

And, as a guest who tries to practice the art of living with others, he will accept and enjoy the favor of his hosts and the company of other guests.

What or how much his host serves to eat and drink will be of no consequence.

Jeeves likes parties.

And, to any invitation that he receives, Jeeves can be counted on to répondez s'il vous plaît.

🐾 ABOVE AVERAGE...

Jeeves came upon a friend on Fifth Street last week.

Jeeves sees his friend often.

But, Jeeves didn't expect to see his friend last week.

His friend's name is Mark Adams,

Mark owns Rancho Roble Vineyards and Winery.

Over the past few weeks, many vineyards have been harvesting grapes.

Last week, Mark was harvesting the grapes from his vineyard.

It's a big job.

Timing is critical when it comes to harvesting any crop, especially grapes.

Although Mark is now a California resident, he was born and raised in Virginia.

Jeeves believes that Mark has an accent.

When Mark speaks, he doesn't sound like other people that Jeeves knows in Lincoln.

He talks more slowly than others.

Some people call Mark's accent a southern drawl.

Mark says, "I may talk slow but I think average."

Jeeves knows that there's nothing average about Mark Adams in thought, in word or in deed.

He's a farmer.

Jeeves believes that farmers are special people.

And, that makes them above average.

They work every day.

They contend with uncertain rainfall like this year's drought or 1997's "pineapple express" that brought floods to northern California.

They contend with uncertain temperatures.

They contend with uncertain soil conditions.

They contend with pests and birds that try to eat their crops.

When Jeeves came upon Mark, he learned that Rancho Roble had not only picked this year's crop, but the crop was already crushed.

And, Rancho Roble's grapes were fermenting.

Mark completed his harvest within two days.

Yet, it will take almost two years before Mark can enjoy wine from the fruit of his labors.

Jeeves drinks water.

He's not old enough to drink wine.

But, many in Jeeves' family drink wine.

They enjoy it.

And, the more they drink wine, the more they seem to enjoy it.

It doesn't matter how much water Jeeves drinks.

He's no more refreshed after ten laps out of his bowl than he is after five laps.

And, water doesn't make him giggle.

Nor does water make him lose his footing.

Nor does water make his face turn crimson.

As a result, Jeeves finds wine interesting.

He's found that it comes in different colors like red, rose and white.

Jeeves understands why some wines are called red.

After all, they're red.

And, Jeeves understands why some wines are called rose.

After all, they're rose.

But, he doesn't know why some wines are called white.

At best, they're pale yellow.

And, he doesn't know why some wines are called dry.

After all, they're wet.

And some wines are called sparkling like prosecco and champagne.

Jeeves doesn't understand those wines at all.

Where are the sparkles?

Jeeves learned that wine dates back almost 8,000 years ("Brief History of Wine," *New York Times,* November 5, 2007).

And, he learned that archeologists found fossils that reveal grape vines from over 60 million years ago.

But Jeeves doesn't know if anyone from the Eocene-age drank wine

Jeeves also learned that Greek historian Thucydides (fifth century B.C.) wrote that "the peoples of the Mediterranean began to emerge from barbarism when they learned to cultivate the olive and the vine."

Placer County Visitors Bureau (visitplacer.com) reports 20 wineries "and counting"

Four of these 20 wineries have Lincoln addresses.

Lincoln wineries include Davis Dean Cellars, Rancho Roble Vineyards and Winery, River Rock Ranch Lindemann Winery and Wise Villa Winery.

If Thucydides was alive today, Jeeves is certain that he would write that Lincoln has emerged from barbarism, even if others may not be so certain.

Regardless, Jeeves believes that all our vintners are above average even if one of them talks "slow."

🐾 A MATTER OF STYLE...

Jeeves has a friend.
Her name is Molly.
She's a neighborhood dog.
Molly gave Jeeves an early Hallowe'en gift.
She gave him a scarf.
It's reversible.
On one side of the scarf, there are ghosts, goblins and pumpkins.
Jeeves will wear this side until October 31.
And, on the other side, there are multicolored hearts.
Jeeves will wear this side after October 31.
Jeeves wears his new scarf tied around his neck.
Sometimes, it's tied so that it falls across his back.
Then, it looks like a cape.
Other times, it's tied so that is falls below his chin.
Then, it looks like a bib.
Jeeves believes his scarf looks fine either way.
But when it falls below his chin, he can see it.
And, it reminds him of Molly.
Thoughts of Molly make Jeeves happy.
Others like to see his scarf across his back.
They believe it's more stylish.
Jeeves doesn't know much about style.
But, he knows what he likes.
And, he knows what he doesn't like.
Scarves come in all shapes, sizes, colors and patterns.
Many wear them in many different ways.
And, many wear them for many different reasons.
Jeeves wonders why they wear scarves.
He wonders how they decide which scarf to pick.
He wonders how they know how to wear a scarf.
He wonders how they know when to wear a scarf.
Jeeves has observed that some pick scarves to match their other clothing.
But, some people pick scarves that don't match at all.
Some loop their scarves twice or more around their necks.
Others let them free-fall.

Some tie them in bows.

Yet, some tie them like a cravat.

Some wear scarves when it's cold.

Yet, some wear them when it's hot.

Jeeves has learned that scarves are as much a fashion accessory as they are a necessity.

And, he's learned that the "why," the "which," the "how," and "when" of scarves is a matter of style.

Jeeves finds style a tricky subject.

Usually style refers to fashion.

But, style is equally important in all types of writing.

Poetry, for example, has many styles.

And different poets are known for different poetic styles.

There's the ballad.

Who can forget Samuel Taylor Coleridge's "Rime of the Ancient Mariner?"

There's the epic.

Who can forget Homer's "Odyssey?"

There's the ode.

Who can forget John Keats' "Ode to a Grecian Urn?"

There's the sonnet.

Who can forget Shakespeare's Sonnet No. 18 "How do I compare thee to a summer's day?"

Jeeves can't remember every poetic line from every one of these poems.

But, he remembers how much joy each poem brings no matter how often he reads them.

There are many more poetry styles.

Some styles are unique to each poet.

E.E. Cummings developed a style that is recognizable as his and his alone.

Jeeves' enjoys poetry.

He looks forward to hearing the results of the annual Voices of Lincoln Poetry Contest.

The 2014 Winners' Event will be held Sunday, October 12 from 3 until 5 p.m. at Lincoln Public Library, 485 Twelve Bridges Drive.

As in prior years, Jeeves knows that he will hear a broad selection of poems from a wide range of poets.

This year, one hundred twenty-seven poets submitted two hundred ninety-seven poems.

The contest attracted entries from forty-four cities in California and from sixteen cities in twelve other states.

Jeeves applauds all poets especially two six-year-olds who are youngest winning poets in this year's contest.

Thirty-five poets, including fifteen young poets (ages 6 through 18), will read forty-two winning poems.

Their poems will represent their thoughts from five topics "One Upon A Time," "Ten Years From Now," "It's A Miracle," "A Journey Worth Taking," and "People Are Funny."

Jeeves can hardly wait to hear these poems.

He wonders if he will hear a ballad.

He wonders if he will hear an epic.

He wonders if he will hear an ode.

He wonders if he will hear a sonnet.

He wonders if he will hear a new style.

And, Jeeves wonders if he will see any poet wear a scarf.

🐾 SCRATCH AND SNIFF...

Jeeves watched the Sept. 13 Lincoln City Council meeting.

He particularly enjoyed Dennis Wagner's presentation from Economic Development Committee.

This committee includes volunteers Rick Bluhm who serves as Chairman, Casey Cloud, James Datzman, Ron Gilman , Judy Guiraud, Richard Pearl, Al Roten, Roger Ueltzen and Dennis Wagner; plus City Councilors Paul Joiner and Stan Nader; and city staff, Jim Estep and Amanda Norton.

Economic Development Committee seeks to increase revenues to the city by attracting new businesses.

During the council meeting, the committee sought approximately $21,000 to help the improve the city's website.

The committee believes that the website is our portal to new business.

So it wants the site to provide accurate information.

While $21,000 may seem like a lot of money, over 200 pages on the city's website need to be updated.

Jeeves doesn't know if that's a competitive price to pay.

But he does know that the city's website needs work.

This week, Jeeves visited the website.

He found a photo of Steve Art.

Steve Art left the city's employ over 6 months ago.

He also found a photo of old city hall posing as new city hall.

New city hall has been open for more than 2 years.

The committee did not exaggerate - the website needs an overhaul.

As a result, Jeeves was troubled by City Council's response to the committee's proposal.

All Councilmen were negative.

Councilman Hydrick's spoke first.

He said that he was disheartened by the committee.

Also, Hydrick chastised it for failing to respond to his email regarding the CCD Expo in Loomis, Sept. 16 to 17.

Jeeves couldn't understand Councilman Hydrick's criticism.

So, Jeeves visited the CCD Expo website, ccdexpo.com.

What he found is interesting.

CCD stands for Content, Creation and Distribution.

The website's link "Who Should Attend" reveals that the expo was designed to attract film makers, producers, videographers and musicians.

Jeeves scratched mightily to find out how an entertainment expo in Loomis helps Lincoln's Economic Development Committee meet the challenge of finding new business revenue anymore than a lingerie convention in Las Vegas or a bungee jumping contest in Podunk.

Jeeves is disheartened by Councilman Hydrick.

Before Councilman Hydrick sends out such emails, Jeeves wonders why he doesn't attempt to gauge their relevance.

By doing so, he might receive responses.

Just because Councilman Hydrick believes that it's a good idea, doesn't mean that it's a good idea.

And just because the Councilman thinks that everyone should think that his idea is a good idea, means that he's arrogant.

But Jeeves is puzzled more by the negative reactions of Mayor Joiner, Councilman Nader and City Manager Estep.

All three serve on the Economic Development Committee.

Jeeves wonders why they didn't raise their concerns during committee meetings.

He also wonders why they would oppose any effort to fix our website that is clearly out of date.

And Jeeves wonders why they waited to trash a proposal from a committee on which they serve and in such a public forum.

While Jeeves understands that the city has no money in its General Fund, he wonders why council failed to suggest other options, such as a grant.

He also wonders why they failed to suggest approaching other businesses that might be willing to help fund the project in cash or in-kind.

If this is a city that can raise $20,000 to fund fireworks that bring in no revenues, why can't it raise a comparable amount to fund a project that helps bring in new revenues?

Jeeves would be willing to donate $100.

He believes that there are others willing to match his contribution.

Jeeves also wonders why City Council failed to suggest reaching out to a university or college and asking students to help with the project as interns.

Nothing positive came from any City Councilman.

And, what troubles Jeeves most is that no City Councilman had the courtesy to say thank you to the committee volunteers.

Jeeves can make no sense out of what he heard.

He suspects that others share his confusion.

So he decided to consult with the Downtown Dogs.

Initially, the dogs were perplexed.

They recognize that Economic Development Committee seeks to find new revenues from outside the city.

That should be a good thing.

They wonder if city council was trying to make way for the report from another committee that seeks to find new revenue from within the city rather than outside - specifically, the Fiscal Sustainability Committee.

After all, the dogs note that Richard Pearl serves on Economic Development Committee and also serves as chairman of the Fiscal Sustainability Committee.

They'd like to know how he can sit and rollover at the same time.

They also wonder if Fiscal Sustainability Committee influenced city council's reaction to Economic Development Committee's proposal.

The Downtown Dogs have detected a whiff of something different in the air.

They believe that it's the odor of a new tax proposal that comes from within.

The odor seems to be emanating from Fiscal Sustainability Committee.

Jeeves and the Downtown Dogs will continue to sniff and scratch.

Eventually, all will be revealed and may even make sense.

Meanwhile, Jeeves would like to publicly thank the Economic Development Committee volunteers for their service and contributions - Chairman Rick Bluhm, Casey Cloud, James Datzman, Ron Gilman , Judy Guiraud, Al Roten, Roger Ueltzen and even Richard Pearl.

But he extends an extra special thanks to committee volunteer, Dennis Wagner, who endured about an hour of abuse from our city council.

The committee volunteers deserve better and they deserve the city's thanks.

And the city deserves better than City Council gave Sept. 13.

🐾 HIS TREE...

Jeeves likes fall.

He enjoys the changes that this season brings.

From his vantage point in Downtown Lincoln, Jeeves watches the colors of the leaves change.

And, he watches the change in shadows that the trees cast as each day grows shorter.

This year, Jeeves mourns the loss of his favorite tree.

It was removed as part of the new downtown street scape.

For eight years, Jeeves watched this tree.

Every year it brought something new to his horizon.

For a few months, the branches would be naked.

Then, signs of new growth would appear.

Little buds, that were almost imperceptible to the naked eye, seemed to magically erupt into deep green leaves.

After a few month months, those leaves started to gradually change color.

They went from deep green to indescribable shades of brilliant red.

At this time of year, Jeeves is reminded of the following poem:

> TREES
> By Joyce Kilmer (August 1913)
>
> I think that I shall never see
> A poem lovely as a tree.
>
> A tree whose hungry mouth is prest
> Against the sweet earth's flowing breast;
>
> A tree that looks at God all day,
> And lifts her leafy arms to pray;
>
> A tree that may in summer wear
> A nest of robins in her hair;
>
> Upon whose bosom snow has lain;
> Who intimately lives with rain.
>
> Poems are made by fools like me,
> But only God can make a tree.

Jeeves now enjoys watching an artist create a new mural on the side of the Family Dollar Store.

By any standards, it's beautiful.

The mural depicts Lincoln's rich history.

Many of the mural's colors are bright and vivid just like the leaves on his favorite tree.

But, unlike leaves on his tree, the mural's colors won't change in the fall.

Instead, they will fade over time.

Jeeves knows that his memory of his tree will also fade over time.

Jeeves still likes the fall.

As he watches the new street scape take shape, Jeeves will continue to mourn the loss of his tree.

But, Jeeves will also enjoy the changes that this season brings to his horizon.

🐾 LIGHTING STRIKES...

Lately, Jeeves has been captivated by our evening skies.

He's seen unusual cloud colors and formations.

He's also seen lightning strikes.

Jeeves learned that some of those lightning strikes caused fires.

Thankfully, Lincoln was spared from another fire.

However, Jeeves believes that our recent skies serve as a metaphor for our city.

In his opinion, Lincoln has three people who are like lightning rods.

They have a tendency to attract negative energy.

It's the kind of energy that causes "fires."

These fires are often difficult to put out.

Jeeves isn't sure what makes them attract such negative energy.

But Jim Estep, Anna Jatczak and Richard Pearl seem to attract higher levels of negativity than other individuals in this city.

They also seems to have ignited more figurative fires than any lightning strikes.

Jeeves has re-read the last 30 months of *Lincoln News Messenger*.

Over and over again, on issue after issue, they seem to be part of news stories disfigured by scorch marks.

Because City Council is responsible for them, it has to put out their fires while it defends their actions.

Three Councilmen learned last week that they no longer have to contend with the burn of a recall that has been smouldering since May.

Jeeves does not believe that the city lightning rods deliberately set out to attract negativity.

Nor does Jeeves believe that they deliberately set out to cause fires.

But the ways in which they execute their duties seem to have a way of igniting fires and creating firestorms.

Yet, all three seem to have many qualifications and much experience.

Perhaps it's solely because of the positions that they hold.

As City Manager, Jim Estep came to town, just over three years ago, to discover bad news - we're broke.

Then, he had to tell us something we didn't want to hear - we're broke.

As Assistant City Manager and CFO, Anna Jatczak, came to town when the city had just discovered its economic woes.

Many taxpayers resented paying for some one new especially when she also told us - we 're broke.

Richard Pearl first came to our attention as a member of the Citizens Advisory Financial Task Force when, as Chairman, he asked for a utility users tax known as Measure K, because - we're broke.

Then, he went on to run for city council and lost.

Recently, he assumed chairmanship of the Fiscal Sustainability Committee.

Jeeves read the Sept. 8 *Lincoln News Messenger* front page ("Fiscal sustainability committee loses first member") and according to former member Chuck Schmidt, the committee plans to propose a new tax.

Jeeves assumes that it's because - we're broke.

"We're broke" is a lousy message to deliver no matter who sends it.

And, Jeeves gets it - we're broke.

He suspects most everyone else gets it too.

He dislikes hearing that we have an ugly baby.

He suspects most everyone else dislikes hearing it too.

He's also tired of hearing the same message.

And, he's tired of hearing it from the same people.

Jeeves would like to hear a different message.

He wants to hear a message that includes new ideas before he hears about a new tax.

And he wants to hear it from someone new.

That's why he was so pleased to hear the Economic Development Committee's proposal during the Sept. 13 council meeting.

Jeeves would like to hear something positive - anything - from city hall.

He was also encouraged when the Fiscal Sustainability Committee was approved by City Council.

Jeeves was pleased to read about the both number and caliber of individuals who volunteered to serve.

The committee seemed to be attracting lot of positive energy.

So he expected something equally positive to come out of their meetings, investigations and deliberations.

But the committee's first order of business was to request the help of outside consultants to facilitate the processes at a cost of $40,000.

He thought that the idea of a volunteer committee meant that the city wouldn't need to spend money for consultants.

Jeeves continues to have reservations about the expenditure of $40,000 for facilitators especially when city council seems unwilling to give Economic Development Committee half that amount in order to fix the city's antiquated website.

For the past few months, Jeeves has decided to adopt a wait and see approach.

He tries to remain hopeful.

But based on recent committee developments, Jeeves is now not so optimistic.

He read that a committee member, Chuck Schmidt, resigned.

Jeeves is troubled by Mr. Schmidt's reasons for doing so (Sept. 15 *Lincoln News Messenger,* A5 "Reader: Fiscal committee leaves sacred cows alone").

He wonders if the committee may be losing its positive energy.

Jeeves hopes that the committee will still be able to gestate new ideas and develop positive solutions.

But despite Richard Pearl's qualifications and good intentions, he will always be associated with an ugly baby.

With a lightning rod at the helm, Jeeves believes that the Fiscal Sustainability Committee may have a tough time bringing their ideas to term and delivering them.

And he believes that it may have an even tougher time getting the public to accept them no matter how much money the committee spends on consultants.

Jeeves will continue to wait and see.

He tries to remain hopeful.

Jeeves knows that just as much as lightning can cause a fire, it can also break through clouds and illuminate a very dark sky.

That's a better metaphor for this great city.

🐾 TO BE OR NOT TO BEE...

Jeeves speaks one language.

He's trying to learn another.

Dog speak is his first language.

This language has no words.

Instead, dog speak consists of noises like barks, growls, howls and whimpers.

Jeeves is trying to learn a second language.

He's trying to learn English.

Jeeves finds that it's a difficult language to learn.

According to the Global Language Monitor (www.languagemonitor.com), the number of English words), now stands at 1,025,109.8.

Jeeves doesn't know which English word accounts for the fraction ".8."

The Global Language Monitor also reports that a new word is created every 98 minutes.

At that rate, Jeeves does not expect to learn all English words in his lifetime.

And, the game of Scrabble will continue to be out of reach.

The few words Jeeves knows, he tries to choose carefully.

And, he tries to use them appropriately.

He doesn't always succeed.

Unlike dog speak, Jeeves finds that the English language is a tricky one.

Last week, he walked passed Lovely Nails on Fifth Street in downtown Lincoln.

He read a sign that showed "Polish Change $6.00."

Jeeves wonders why Polish want to change.

If so, what would they become?

And, why they would change for a mere $6.00?

Jeeves wouldn't become anything else but American no matter how little or how much it cost to change.

He asked the Downtown Dogs "why Polish want to change?"

They explained to Jeeves that the sign was referring to the lacquer that goes on finger or toe nails not the Polish nationality.

They went on to explain that, in the case of finger and toe nails, polish is pronounced like polish.

When it comes to the Polish nationality, the word is pronounced like polish.

Jeeves was relieved to learn that the Polish are not looking to change although he hopes they want to be Americans too.

So, from the dogs, Jeeves learned that there are English words, like Polish and polish, that are spelled the same but sound differently and have different meanings.

These types of words are called heteronyms.

And, from the dogs, he learned that there are English words, like soared and sword, that are spelled differently and sound the same but have different meanings.

These types of words are called homonyms, or more specifically, homophones.

If that wasn't enough, from the dogs Jeeves learned that there are English words, like incense, that are spelled the same, may sound the same but have different meanings.

These types of words are called homographs.

Jeeves wonders how anyone learns English.

It's confusing when so many English words sound alike but mean something different.

For that reason, Jeeves applauds students like Tyler Baser.

Tyler is a fourth grade student at Lincoln's Carlin C. Coppin Elementary School.

Recently, he and five other students from Western Placer Unified School District qualified to participate, as finalists, in the 2015 Placer County Spelling Bee.

Jeeves saw Tyler on KQCA My58's March 12, 2015 10 p.m. newscast.

Many thousands of Placer County's students competed first in their schools.

However, just 74 became finalists for the recent county-wide competition in Rocklin.

Tyler made it to the third round before being disqualified.

Jeeves is proud of Tyler Baser.

But, no one is more proud of Tyler than his grandmother Della Ramsey.

Jeeves also saw her on the KQCA newscast.

Della was a member of the audience.

She was also the first to tell Jeeves about the spelling bee and kept him up-to-date on his progress.

Many readers of this blog may know Della too.

She is one of the great crew at Simple Pleasures Restaurant and Catering.

Jeeves is equally proud of the other students from our school district.

Their names are Dante Campos, Sophia Lee, Jay Marston, Erik McManny and Layla Ward.

English remains a tricky second language for Jeeves to learn.

It's doubtful that he'll ever know enough to participate in a spelling bee.

Happily, the English language is less complicated for Tyler Baser and at least 73 other Placer County spelling bee competitors.

And, that's an accomplishment in any language.

It's enough to make Jeeves bark - like a dog not a tree.

🐾 MUTT AND JEFF...

Before spending most of his time with the Downtown Dogs, Jeeves used to spend a lot of time with Jeff Greenberg.

Jeff is a familiar face to many Lincoln residents.

Some know Jeff as a volunteer at the Twelve Bridges Library book sales.

Some know Jeff as the man on his hands and knees praying that City of Lincoln would be selected All American City.

Some know Jeff as an umpire at the Del Webb softball games.

Some know Jeff as the guy who stands in the pool at Orchard Creek.

Some know Jeff as a regular diet coke drinker in the Sports Bar.

Some know Jeff as the driver of a yellow and white golf cart.

Some know Jeff as the candidate for city council.

Some know Jeff as the contestant who dressed up as a woman for *Lincoln's Got Talent*.

Some know Jeff as the man in black track pants who calls himself "big and loud."

But Jeeves knows Jeff in other ways.

He knows Jeff who as the man responsible for putting on the very best events in downtown Lincoln.

Remember RibFest?

Remember ItalianFest?

Alas, Jeff dissolved his non profit organization called Friends of Lincoln Kids.

Jeff's events will be no more.

Jeeves mourns the loss of Jeff's great events.

And now that Jeff doesn't put on events, he doesn't spend as much time in downtown Lincoln.

That's a shame because downtown Lincoln needs people like Jeff.

Jeeves misses chewing the fat with Jeff.

And, he misses Jeff's genuine enthusiasm for this city.

Jeeves also knows Jeff as the man who said that Jeeves should write a blog instead of a weekly newspaper column.

At the time, Jeeves didn't understand what he meant.

Jeff explained to Jeeves that he needed a web site in order to have a blog.

Jeeves wondered why Jeff would send him after something built by a spider.

While he knew where to find plenty of cobwebs, Jeeves couldn't connect them to a blog.

A blog sounded like a cross between and a blob and a frog.

How could that be good?

Rather than chase his tail, Jeeves met with the Downtown Dogs around the fountain in Beermann Plaza.

Together, they finally figured out what Jeff Greenberg meant.

But creating a blog was beyond their expertise.

Besides none of the dogs had access to a computer.

Undeterred, they sniffed around until they found someone to help.

Which brings us here today.

Jeeves would like to thank Jeff Greenberg for inspiring this blog and for all that he has done for this wonderful city.

Jeeves and all the Downtown Dogs will be happy to set aside a place for Jeff around the fountain in Beermann Plaza on one condition.

He can't dress up as a woman.

🐾 LAST FOR BEST...

Jeeves is grateful.

He's grateful to Nasha the Scottie.

She wrote last week's blog for him.

And, Jeeves is excited.

He's excited about what he discovered when he read Nasha's blog.

She wrote about the Bookfair that Friends of Lincoln Library and Barnes & Noble will hold from Thursday, October 15 until Saturday, October 20, 2015.

A percentage of all book purchases will go to Friends of Lincoln Library.

But, buyers must remember to take a copy of a voucher.

Or, buyers may give the Bookfair identification number when they check out.

Barnes & Noble is located in Roseville at the Creekside Town Center, 1256 Galleria Boulevard.

Jeeves can hardly wait to meet Mother Goose on Saturday, October 17.

She will be available from 10 a.m. until 2 p.m.

Jeeves plans to have his picture taken with her.

And, he will make another trip to Barnes & Noble on Sunday, October 18

This time, Jeeves can hardly wait to meet Jeri Chase Ferris.

Jeri is an award- winning author of children's books and will be on hand from 11:00 a.m. until 1:00 p.m.

Jeri Chase Ferris makes history come alive.

Besides *Noah Webster and His Words,* she has written about Harriet Tubman in *Go Free or Die,* Thomas Jefferson in *Thomas Jefferson: Father of Liberty,* Sojourner Truth in *Walking the Road to Freedom,* plus many other books about important people who have shaped this nation.

Jeeves plans to purchase more of Jeri's books.

And, he hopes that she will autograph them.

Nasha is excited too.

Like Jeeves, she looks forward to meeting Mother Goose.

And, she has a list of books that she wants to add to her collection.

Both Nasha and Jeeves will take their vouchers.

They want to support to Friends of Lincoln Library during this week's Bookfair.

Although he's excited about the Bookfair, Jeeves is also apprehensive about next week.

He doesn't know what he's going to do with his free time.

Of course, Jeeves will enjoy reading his new books.

And, he still has a few old bones to dig up and some new bones to bury.

But, he won't have his blog any longer.

Last week, Jeeves received disturbing news from his webmaster.

The webmaster wrote "For some reason, your site keeps being picked on by hackers. We are not having this problem on any of our other sites. Not sure why your site keeps getting attacked so hard. I have 15 other sites and it takes about 30 minutes a month to manage all of them, while Jeeves averages 3-4 hours and last night was almost 5 hours alone."

Despite the constant attention of its webmaster, Jeeves' website has become too difficult and too expensive to manage and maintain.

Jeeves is just a little dog.

As such, his blog is little too.

And, it has an even smaller budget.

Like his webmaster, Jeeves has no idea either why his site keeps being picked on or by whom.

Although he enjoys writing his weekly blog, Jeeves is unwilling to subject his readers to potential threats that may come to their computers by means of his website.

And, he is equally unwilling to subject his good friend and webmaster to more demands on his time.

Jeeves is disappointed that hackers interfere and disrupt our daily lives.

He wishes that they would spend their time on more worthwhile pursuits.

Alas, theirs is a pitiful existence.

Jeeves didn't expect early retirement.

After all, he's only seven.

In people years, that's about 42.

But, now that retirement is here, Jeeves will spend his time differently.

Unlike hackers, he will try to be productive.

Jeeves will read more.

He's happy to have Barnes & Noble nearby.

And, he's even happier to have a library in Lincoln from which he can borrow books.

But, Jeeves is happiest to have Friends of Lincoln Library who make sure that Lincoln's library stays open.

www.ingramcontent.com/pod-product-compliance
Lightning Source LLC
Chambersburg PA
CBHW022101090426
42743CB00008B/684